MOVIE ★ ICONS

GRANT

EDITOR
PAUL DUNCAN

TEXT
F. X. FEENEY

PHOTOS
THE KOBAL COLLECTION

TASCHEN

HONG KONG KÖLN LONDON LOS ANGELES MADRID PARIS TOKYO

CONTENTS

Kodak
37
36
35
34
33
32
NORTH SHORE
LIMITED
PARCEL ROOM
GO BY TRAIN

ICE
BUILDING
ENT A

1

CARY GRANT: CHARMING MAN

BY F. X. FEENEY

DER CHARMEUR

GENTLEMAN

CARY GRANT: CHARMING MAN

by F. X. Feeney

He is the most self-invented man in movies, this side of Charlie Chaplin.

Indeed, both escaped poverty by training as acrobats. One can argue that Chaplin's Tramp and Cary Grant's Cosmopolitan are, artistically, father and son. Both are gentlemen, both brim with confidence, both are deeply romantic, and funny – but the younger one has a better tailor.

Pauline Kael caught Grant's beauty in action when she called him 'The Man from Dream City.' His air of seeming equal to every occasion was a studied illusion – and years in the making. In the early 1930s, Paramount Pictures cast him in an uncertain variety of mysteries and romances (among them, Josef von Sternberg's excellent *Blonde Venus* (1932), which starred Marlene Dietrich) not to mention two comedies opposite Mae West. The former Archie Leach of Bristol, England, paid close attention to everything that worked best about himself onscreen, and patiently eliminated everything that didn't – forging 'Cary Grant'. When his Paramount contract lapsed in 1936, he took the reins of his career, signing only semi-exclusive agreements with Columbia Studios and RKO, and otherwise working freelance. He was the first film star ever to do this. Thus begins the career for which he is remembered.

In *The Awful Truth* (1937), directed by Leo McCarey – an urbane man from whom he is said to have copied his clipped, trademark manner – Grant suavely conceals his still-burning passion for ex-wife Irene Dunne, backhandedly wooing her by pretending to push her into the clumsy arms of Ralph Bellamy. He does the same to Rosalind Russell in *His Girl Friday* (1940) for director Howard Hawks, once again using Bellamy as a foil – and makes a similar (if more sophisticated) stooge of James Stewart to win back ex-wife Katharine Hepburn in *The Philadelphia Story* (1940).

Grant was never afraid to *seem* to repeat himself, trusting his forceful, innate spontaneity to make each moment new. This made him ideal for directors like Hawks and Alfred

"You say everybody wants to be Cary Grant? Even I want to be Cary Grant."
Cary Grant

Hitchcock, who relished any chance to revitalize old formulas and set pieces. His impeccable timing and light, cat-burglar's touch at stealing women's hearts were perfect for the jaunty heroics and romantic farce of such Hawks fare as *Bringing Up Baby* (1938), *Only Angels Have Wings* (1939), and *Monkey Business* (1952). The sometimes sinister amoral cool which shadowed his great charm lent itself well to the high suspense (often laced with subtle comedy) of Hitchcock. Although the popular Grant persona reversed the downbeat ending originally planned for *Suspicion* (1941) – audiences would not have tolerated seeing him exposed as a killer – actor and director rebounded a few years later with a sexier, more successful ambiguity opposite Ingrid Bergman in *Notorious* (1946).

At age 9, he was told his mother was dead – the great trauma of his childhood. At age 29, he learned the opposite, that his mother had been locked away (apparently unjustly) in a mental hospital – and this became the great trauma of his adult life. He rescued her, though her mind had been mostly destroyed by her incarceration, and saw to her wellbeing for the next 40 years. Only once did his movies touch directly on such pain, in the mother-son relationship sensitively portrayed by writer-director Clifford Odets in *None But the Lonely Heart* (1944). That film's box-office failure steered Grant away from ever opening such a vein again, except on the sly, as he had earlier in the elegant tearjerker *Penny Serenade* (1941) and its later twin, *An Affair to Remember* (1957). One fine offbeat variation on the mythic Grant persona is to be found in *Crisis* (1950), written and directed by Richard Brooks. It is a thriller with a political bite, in which Grant is a vacationing surgeon held hostage by a South American dictator (José Ferrer) who needs a brain operation. Otherwise, look to *North by Northwest* (1959), Hitchcock's superb madcap thriller (direct ancestor of all 007 films), in which Grant is mistaken for someone else so fiercely and repeatedly that the only way that he can save himself is to pretend to be that person. If ever a film could be said to represent the whole mystery of Cary Grant, however playfully, it is this one.

He made other good pictures – *Charade* (1963), *Father Goose* (1964) – but by then years of therapy and the prospect of new fatherhood in 1966 liberated him from playing 'Cary Grant'. He was free at last to retire, and simply *be* Cary Grant. The role became the man, in the most life-giving sense. One could wish no man greater happiness than that.

ENDPAPERS/VORSATZBLATT/PAGE DE GARDE
STILL FROM 'NORTH BY NORTHWEST' (1959)

PAGES 2/3
CARY GRANT & RANDOLPH SCOTT (1933)

PAGE 4
PORTRAIT FOR 'INDISCREET' (1958)

PAGES 6/7
ON THE SET OF 'NORTH BY NORTHWEST' (1959)

PAGE 8
PORTRAIT (1942)

OPPOSITE/RECHTS/CI-CONTRE
STILL FROM 'CHARADE' (1963)

CARY GRANT: DER CHARMEUR

von F. X. Feeney

Seit Charlie Chaplin gab es wohl keinen anderen Mann im Filmgeschäft, der sich in solchem Maße selbst ‚erfand' wie Cary Grant. Tatsächlich entkamen beide ihren ärmlichen Verhältnissen, indem sie Akrobatik erlernten. Man könnte sogar behaupten, dass Chaplins Tramp und Grants Weltbürger – künstlerisch gesehen – Vater und Sohn sind. Beide sind Gentlemen, beide stecken voller Selbstvertrauen, beide sind zutiefst romantisch und außerdem komisch – nur dass der Junior einen besseren Schneider hatte.

Pauline Kael brachte Grants schauspielerische Größe auf den Punkt, als sie ihn den ‚Mann aus der Traumstadt' nannte. Sein Auftreten, mit dem er vorgab, jeder Situation gewachsen zu sein, war eine gut einstudierte Illusion, an der er jahrelang gefeilt hatte. Anfang der dreißiger Jahre des letzten Jahrhunderts setzte ihn Paramount Pictures in einer Reihe von Kriminal- und Liebesfilmen ein (darunter *Blonde Venus* [1932] von Josef von Sternberg, mit Marlene Dietrich in der Hauptrolle) sowie in zwei Komödien an der Seite von Mae West. Der ehemalige Archie Leach aus dem englischen Bristol achtete sehr genau darauf, was an ihm auf der Leinwand am besten wirkte, und verwarf nach und nach all das, was nicht funktionierte. Auf diese Weise schmiedete er geduldig seinen ‚Cary Grant'. Als der Vertrag mit Paramount 1936 auslief, nahm er seine Karriere selbst in die Hand und schloss offene Vereinbarungen mit Columbia und RKO, die ihm ermöglichten, nebenher noch selbständig zu arbeiten. Er war der erste Filmstar, dem dies gelang. So begann die Karriere, mit der er in Erinnerung blieb.

Man sagt Grant nach, er habe sich seine charakteristisch kurzangebundene Art bei dem eleganten und weltmännischen Regisseur Leo McCarey abgeschaut. Unter dessen Regie spielte er in *Die schreckliche Wahrheit* (1937) einen Mann, der seine noch immer glühende Leidenschaft für seine Ex-Frau (Irene Dunne) geschickt verbirgt und sie indirekt umwirbt, indem er vorgibt, sie dem unbeholfenen Dan (Ralph Bellamy) in die Arme zu treiben. Das Gleiche versuchte er erneut mit Hildy (Rosalind Russell) in *Sein Mädchen für besondere Fälle* (1940) unter der Regie von Howard Hawks und wieder mit Bellamy als Nebenbuhler – und ähnlich behandelte er auch den etwas raffinierteren Macauley (James Stewart), um seine Ex-Frau Tracy (Katharine Hepburn) in *Die Nacht vor der Hochzeit* (1940) zurückzugewinnen.

STILL FROM 'CHARADE' (1963)
Iconic Cary Grant – wit of a Don Juan, heart of a clown. / Cary Grant, die Ikone – mit dem Witz eines Don Juan und dem Herzen eines Clowns. / Cary Grant tel qu'en lui-même : un esprit de séducteur, un cœur de clown.

„Sie behaupten, jeder wäre gerne Cary Grant? Sogar ich wäre gerne Cary Grant!"
Cary Grant

Grant scheute sich nie vor solchen *vermeintlichen* Wiederholungen, denn er vertraute auf die Wirkung seiner angeborenen Spontaneität, die jede Szene neu und frisch erscheinen ließ. Damit war er eine Idealbesetzung für Regisseure wie Howard Hawks und Alfred Hitchcock, die mit Vorliebe alte Formeln und Versatzstücke mit neuem Leben füllten. Sein unfehlbares Timing und seine lockere Art, wie ein heranschleichender Dieb in der Nacht die Herzen der Frauen zu stehlen, passten ideal zu Hawks' frechen Heldenstückchen und romantischen Komödien wie etwa *Leoparden küßt man nicht* (1938), *SOS Feuer an Bord* (1939) und *Liebling, ich werde jünger* (1952). Und die mitunter düstere amoralische Abgebrühtheit, die ihren Schatten über seinen enormen Charme warf, war wie geschaffen für die (oft mit subtilem Humor versetzte) Hochspannung bei Hitchcock. Obwohl Grants populäres Image Anlass dazu gab, den ursprünglich für *Verdacht* (1941) vorgesehenen Schluss ins Gegenteil zu verkehren – das Publikum hätte nicht geduldet, dass man ihn als Mörder überführt –, schufen der Regisseur und Schauspieler ein paar Jahre später einen verführerischen und sehr viel mehrdeutigeren Charakter neben Ingrid Bergman in *Berüchtigt*.

Im Alter von neun Jahren erzählte man Archie, seine Mutter sei tot – es war das große Trauma seiner Kindheit. Mit 29 fand er dann die Wahrheit heraus: dass seine Mutter (offenbar zu Unrecht) in einer Nervenklinik eingesperrt worden war – und diese Tatsache wurde zum großen Trauma seines Erwachsenenlebens. Er holte sie aus der Anstalt, doch die vielen Jahre hinter Gittern hatten sie geistig und seelisch zermürbt. Während der nächsten vierzig Jahre sorgte er für ihr Wohlergehen. Nur ein einziges Mal rührte einer seiner Filme unmittelbar an diese offene Wunde, und zwar in der Beziehung zwischen Mutter und Sohn, die der Regisseur und Dramatiker Clifford Odets in *None But the Lonely Heart* (1944) so einfühlsam darstellt. Der kommerzielle Misserfolg dieses Films veranlasste Grant, solche Stoffe fortan allenfalls zu streifen, so wie er es in dem eleganten Rührstück *Akkorde der Liebe* (1941) bereits getan hatte und später in dem ähnlichen *Die große Liebe meines Lebens* (1957) abermals tat. Eine ebenso gelungene wie ausgefallene Variante der mythischen Grant-Rolle findet man in *Hexenkessel* (1950) nach dem Drehbuch und unter der Regie von Richard Brooks. Es handelt sich um einen Thriller mit politischem Biss, in dem Grant einen Chirurgen auf Urlaub spielt, der von einem südamerikanischen Diktator (José Ferrer) als Geisel gehalten wird, weil dieser dringend einer Hirnoperation bedarf. Ansonsten sollte man sich *Der unsichtbare Dritte* (1959) anschauen, Hitchcocks herausragende Verfolgungsjagd (der unmittelbare Vorfahre aller 007-Filme), bei der Grant als Roger Thornhill so hartnäckig und unentwegt von allen verwechselt wird, dass er sich nur retten kann, indem er tatsächlich in die Rolle dieser Person schlüpft. Wenn es irgendeinen Film gibt, der das ganze Geheimnis von Cary Grant auf den Punkt bringt – und sei es auch noch so verspielt –, dann ist es dieser.

Er drehte noch weitere gute Filme – *Charade* (1963), *Der große Wolf ruft* (1964) –, aber dann befreite er sich nach langjähriger Therapie im Jahr 1966 von der Verpflichtung ‚Cary Grant' zu spielen und blickte einer erneuten Vaterschaft entgegen. Endlich konnte er sich zur Ruhe setzen und einfach nur Cary Grant *sein*. Er machte sich seine Rolle im wirklichen Leben zu eigen und gab ihr dadurch größtmöglichen Sinn. Ein größeres Glück kann man niemandem wünschen.

STILL FROM 'ARSENIC AND OLD LACE' (1944)
Lethal hijinks opposite Raymond Massey and Peter Lorre. / Spielchen mit tödlichem Ausgang – neben Raymond Massey und Peter Lorre. / Fatales pitreries en compagnie de Raymond Massey et de Peter Lorre.

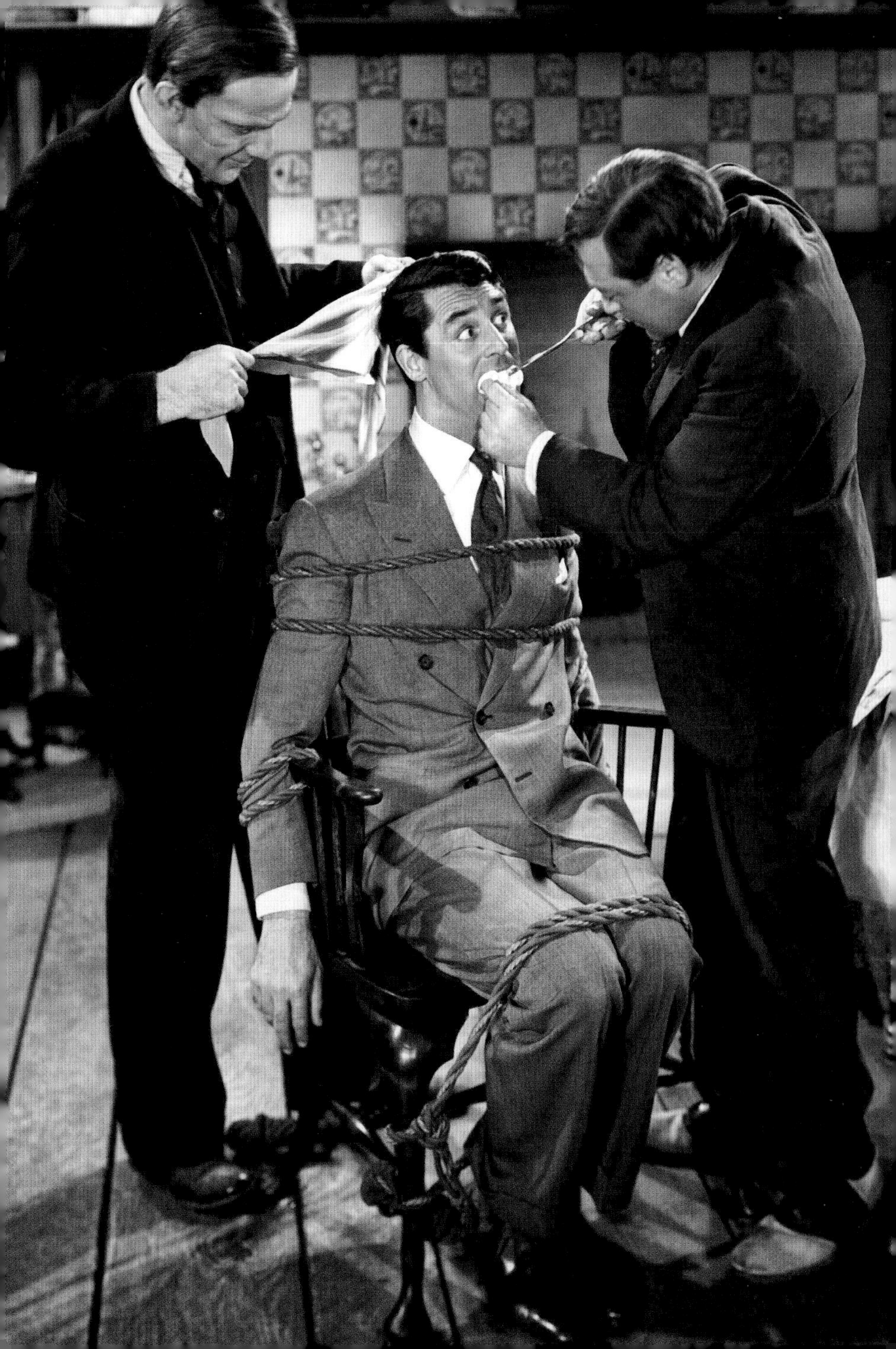

CARY GRANT : GENTLEMAN

F. X. Feeney

De toute l'histoire du cinéma, c'est sans doute l'acteur qui s'est le plus inventé de toutes pièces – avec Charlie Chaplin, bien sûr.

Comme Chaplin, Grant a échappé à la pauvreté en s'engageant dans une troupe d'acrobates. D'un point de vue artistique, le vagabond de Chaplin et le personnage cosmopolite de Grant sont comme père et fils. Tous deux sont des gentlemen débordants d'assurance, profondément romantiques et drôles – même si le plus jeune possède un meilleur tailleur.

La célèbre critique Pauline Kael a bien cerné le charme de Cary Grant en le surnommant « L'Homme rêveur ». Le flegme dont il ne se défait en aucune circonstance est une pause soigneusement étudiée, qu'il a mis des années à peaufiner. Au début des années 1930, la Paramount le fait jouer dans un nombre incalculable de films mystérieux ou sentimentaux (dont l'excellent *La Vénus blonde* (1932) de Josef von Sternberg, avec Marlene Dietrich), sans oublier ses deux comédies avec Mae West. À force d'étudier les détails qui passent le mieux à l'écran et d'éliminer patiemment tout le reste, Archie Leach, natif de Bristol, donne peu à peu naissance au personnage de Cary Grant. Quand son contrat avec la Paramount arrive à échéance en 1936, il prend sa carrière en mains, signant des contrats semi-exclusifs avec Columbia et RKO et travaillant par ailleurs en indépendant. Il est le premier à agir de la sorte, et c'est le début de la carrière que l'on sait.

Dans *Cette sacrée vérité* (1937), réalisé par Leo McCarey – homme courtois auquel il aurait emprunté sa célèbre diction saccadée –, Grant masque sa passion encore brûlante pour son ex-femme Irene Dunne, qu'il courtise indirectement en feignant de la pousser dans les bras maladroits de Ralph Bellamy. Il en fait de même avec Rosalind Russell dans *La Dame du vendredi* (1940) de Howard Hawks, utilisant à nouveau Bellamy comme repoussoir. Dans *Indis-*

STILL FROM 'HOLIDAY' (1938)
Katharine Hepburn, his match in intellect and charm. / Katharine Hepburn war ihm in Intellekt und Charme durchaus ebenbürtig. / Katharine Hepburn, son égale par l'intellect et par le charme.

« Je n'ai aucun regret. Je n'aurais pas vécu comme je l'ai fait si je me souciais du qu'en-dira-t-on. »
Cary Grant

crétions (1940), c'est James Stewart qui lui sert de faire-valoir (avec certes plus de classe) pour reconquérir son ex-femme, interprétée par Katharine Hepburn.

Grant ne craint jamais d'avoir l'air de se répéter, car sa spontanéité innée insuffle à chaque scène un vent de nouveauté. Cela fait de lui un acteur idéal pour des cinéastes comme Howard Hawks et Alfred Hitchcock, toujours avides de renouveler les vieilles formules et les figures imposées. Son impeccable sens du rythme et la légèreté avec laquelle il dérobe le cœur de ces dames conviennent parfaitement à la bravoure guillerette et à la bouffonnerie romantique de films de Howard Hawks tels que *L'Impossible Monsieur Bébé* (1938), *Seuls les anges ont des ailes* (1939) et *Chérie, je me sens rajeunir* (1952). De même, le détachement un brin sinistre qui obscurcit parfois son charme irrésistible s'accorde à merveille au suspense haletant (souvent empreint d'une pointe d'humour subtil) qu'affectionne Hitchcock. Bien que la popularité du personnage de Cary Grant l'ait contraint à renoncer au dénouement pessimiste initialement prévu pour *Soupçons* (1941) – le public n'aurait pas supporté de voir en lui un assassin –, Hitchcock se rattrape quelques années plus tard en lui confiant un rôle plus profondément et plus érotiquement ambigu face à Ingrid Bergman dans *Les Enchaînés* (1946).

À l'âge de 9 ans, on lui annonce que sa mère est morte, ce qui provoque en lui un profond traumatisme. À 29 ans, il apprend qu'elle est vivante et a été internée (apparemment à tort) dans un asile psychiatrique, ce qui le traumatise à nouveau. Il vole à sa rescousse, malgré les graves séquelles laissées par son internement, et veille à son bien-être pendant 40 ans. Il n'évoquera ouvertement ce drame qu'une seule fois dans sa carrière, avec la relation mère-fils délicatement dépeinte par l'auteur et réalisateur Clifford Odets dans *Rien qu'un cœur solitaire* (1944). L'échec commercial du film dissuadera Cary Grant de puiser à nouveau dans cette veine, sinon à la dérobée, comme il l'a déjà fait dans l'élégant mélo *La Chanson du passé* (1941) et le refera dans *Elle et lui* (1957). Une variante originale du personnage mythique de Cary Grant apparaît dans *Cas de conscience* (1950), écrit et réalisé par Richard Brooks. Dans ce thriller à consonance politique, il incarne un chirurgien pris en otage par un dictateur sud-américain (José Ferrer) atteint d'une tumeur au cerveau. Notons également *La Mort aux trousses* (1959), thriller haletant de Hitchcock (et ancêtre direct des films de James Bond), où Cary Grant est pris pour un autre avec un tel acharnement qu'il finit par se faire passer pour lui afin de sauver sa peau. Si un film exprime le mystère de Cary Grant, fût-ce avec humour, c'est bien celui-là.

D'autres bons films suivront, tels *Charade* (1963) et *Grand méchant loup appelle* (1964), mais en 1966, des ans de psychanalyse et la perspective de la paternité le libèrent du besoin de jouer « Cary Grant ». Enfin libre de prendre sa retraite, il se contentera désormais d'*être* Cary Grant. Le personnage s'est fait homme, prenant réellement vie. Quel plus grand bonheur peut-on souhaiter à un homme ?

PAGE 22

PORTRAIT (1933)
'Star persona' as yet unformed, but oozing pure potential. / Noch war seine Rolle als „Star" nicht ganz ausgereift, doch Grants Potential war unübersehbar. / Une star encore en gestation, mais au potentiel débordant.

PORTRAIT FOR 'HOUSEBOAT' (1958)
Ever cool, even in the volcanic embrace of Sophia Loren. / Immer ganz cool – sogar in den Armen der feurigen Sophia Loren. / Un homme qui sait garder son sang-froid, même dans les bras de la volcanique Sophia Loren.

2

VISUAL FILMOGRAPHY

FILMOGRAFIE IN BILDERN
FILMOGRAPHIE EN IMAGES

MAN IN A SUIT

MANN IM ANZUG

UN PARFAIT GENTLEMAN

STILL FROM 'SINGAPORE SUE' (1932)
An early, uncredited cameo as a raucous Cockney sailor. / Ein früher Auftritt ohne Namensnennung als rauher Seemann mit Cockney-Akzent. / Sa première apparition, non créditée, dans le rôle d'un marin mal dégrossi.

"My father used to say, 'Let them see you and not the suit. That should be secondary.'"
Cary Grant

„Mein Vater pflegte zu sagen: ‚Sieh zu, dass sie dich sehen und nicht deinen Anzug. Der sollte zweitrangig sein.'"
Cary Grant

« Mon père disait toujours : "C'est toi qu'on doit voir, pas ton costume. Le reste, c'est secondaire." »
Cary Grant

STILL FROM 'THIS IS THE NIGHT' (1932)
Smoothly romancing Lily Damita in his first feature outing. / In seiner ersten richtigen Spielfilmrolle umgarnt er Lily Damita. / En train de courtiser Lily Damita dans son premier long métrage.

STILL FROM 'SINNERS IN THE SUN' (1932)
One of many wooing adulterous Carole Lombard. / Einer von vielen Freiern, der einer Ehebrecherin (Carole Lombard) den Hof macht. / L'un des nombreux prétendants de la volage Carole Lombard.

STILL FROM 'MERRILY WE GO TO HELL' (1932)
Waltzing Adrienne Ames in a powdered wig, for a stage-play. / Mit gepuderter Perücke schiebt er in einem Bühnenstück Adrienne Ames im Walzertakt über das Parkett. / Valsant avec Adrienne Ames, en perruque poudrée, lors d'une représentation théâtrale.

"It takes 500 small details to add up to one favorable impression."
Cary Grant

„Fünfhundert kleine Details machen zusammen einen guten Eindruck."
Cary Grant

« Il faut 500 petits détails pour faire une bonne impression. »
Cary Grant

STILL FROM 'DEVIL AND THE DEEP' (1932)
'The other man' wooing Tallulah Bankhead from Charles Laughton. / Der ‚Andere', der dem Kommandanten (Charles Laughton) die Ehefrau (Tallulah Bankhead) ausspannen will. / Dans le rôle du rival tentant de séduire Tallulah Bankhead, l'épouse de Charles Laughton.

STILL FROM 'BLONDE VENUS' (1932)
Yet another 'other man,' this time seducing Marlene Dietrich. / Und wieder in der Rolle des ‚anderen Mannes', diesmal als Verführer von Marlene Dietrich. / Encore dans le rôle du rival, cette fois en train de séduire Marlene Dietrich.

PAGES 30/31
STILL FROM 'BLONDE VENUS' (1932)
Director Josef von Sternberg framed the pair with characteristic elegance. / Regisseur Josef von Sternberg setzte das Paar mit charakteristischer Eleganz in Szene. / Cadrés avec l'élégance caractéristique du metteur en scène Josef von Sternberg.

RIGHT/RECHTS/CI-CONTRE

STILL FROM 'HOT SATURDAY' (1932)

With Nancy Carroll, once again as the extra man in a love triangle. / Mit Nancy Carroll – wieder einmal als der „dritte Mann" in einer Dreiecksbeziehung. / L'éternel rival dans un triangle amoureux avec Nancy Carroll.

PAGES 34/35

STILL FROM 'SHE DONE HIM WRONG' (1933)

Mae West specifically requested Grant for the lead. / Mae West bat ausdrücklich darum, dass Grant die Hauptrolle erhielt. / Mae West l'a spécifiquement réclamé pour le premier rôle.

LOBBY CARD FOR 'MADAME BUTTERFLY' (1932)

With Sylvia Sydney, superb (in a non-singing role) as Puccini's geisha. / Mit Sylvia Sydney, die (in einer gesanglosen Rolle) Puccinis Geisha ausgezeichnet verkörpert. / Avec Sylvia Sydney, superbe (dans un rôle non chanté) en geisha de Puccini.

LA
BELLE
NIDIA

LOBBY CARD FOR 'THE WOMAN ACCUSED' (1933)

Nancy Carroll is his co-star in this quirky shipboard comedy-drama. / In einem originellen Drama mit Nancy Carroll an seiner Seite. / En croisière avec Nancy Carroll dans une comédie dramatique excentrique.

STILL FROM 'THE EAGLE AND THE HAWK' (1933)

Opposite Frederic March (right) in this drama of World War One. / Neben Frederic March (rechts) in einem Drama, das im Ersten Weltkrieg spielt. / Aux côtés de Frederic March (à droite) dans un drame sur la Première Guerre mondiale.

STILL FROM 'GAMBLING SHIP' (1933)
A con-man posing as a tycoon, opposite Eleanor LaVelle, who has her own agenda. / Ein Hochstapler gibt sich als Tycoon aus – mit Eleanor LaVelle (Benita Hume), die eigene Pläne verfolgt. / En escroc se faisant passer pour un riche homme d'affaires auprès d'Eleanor LaVelle, qui ne joue pas franc jeu non plus.

ADVERT FOR 'I'M NO ANGEL' (1933)
Their successful pairing in 'She Done Him Wrong' made a rematch inevitable. / Das erfolgreiche Gespann in *Sie tat ihm unrecht* schrie geradezu nach Wiederholung. / Leur succès dans *Lady Lou* rendait une nouvelle collaboration inévitable.

She takes GRANT

ike GRANT took RICHMOND!

MAE WEST in "I'M NO ANGEL"
with CARY GRANT
directed by Wesley Ruggles

it's a PARAMOUNT PICTURE, it's the best show in town!

STILL FROM 'I'M NO ANGEL' (1933)
"Oh," West tells him (having written the film), "I'm very quick in a slow way." / „Oh", meint West (die den Film selbst geschrieben hat) zu ihm, „ich bin sehr schnell, wenn man es langsam angeht." / « Je comprends vite quand on m'explique lentement », confie Mae West (qui a coécrit le scénario).

PORTRAIT FOR 'I'M NO ANGEL' (1933)
"You fascinate me," Mae West warns Cary: "You'd better go." / „Du faszinierst mich", warnt Tira (Mae West) Jack (Grant). „Es ist besser, wenn du gehst." / Mae West avertit Cary : « Vous me fascinez. Vous feriez mieux de partir. »

STILL FROM 'THIRTY DAY PRINCESS' (1934)
Sylvia Sidney in a double role, as both a princess and her imposter. / Sylvia Sidney in einer Doppelrolle als Prinzessin und Hochstaplerin. / Sylvia Sidney dans le double rôle de la princesse et de son sosie.

PORTRAIT FOR 'ALICE IN WONDERLAND' (1933)
Is that a steer or a turtle? In any case, Cary Grant is inside – we're told. / Ist es ein Ochse oder eine Schildkröte? Im Kostüm steckt jedenfalls Cary Grant – heißt es. / Bœuf ou tortue ? Quoi qu'il en soit, il paraît que Cary Grant est dedans.

STILL FROM 'BORN TO BE BAD' (1934)
Momentarily enamored of a wayward, scheming mother (Loretta Young). / Einen Augenblick lang ist er von der unberechenbaren und intriganten Mutter (Loretta Young) angetan. / Momentanément épris d'une mère volage et intrigante (Loretta Young).

STILL FROM 'KISS AND MAKE-UP' (1934)
In this satire on cosmetic surgery, Grant makes a faux-goddess out of Genevieve Tobin. / In dieser Satire auf die kosmetische Chirurgie verwandelt ein Arzt (Grant) Eve (Genevieve Tobin) in eine Retortenschönheit. / Dans cette satire sur la chirurgie esthétique, Grant transforme Genevieve Tobin en déesse factice.

STILL FROM 'LADIES SHOULD LISTEN' (1934)
A target of several women (among them Frances Drake, kissed here) and blackmail. / Für mehrere Frauen (darunter Frances Drake, die er hier küsst) und Erpresser wird er zur Zielscheibe. / La cible de plusieurs femmes (ici Frances Drake en train de l'embrasser) et d'un maître chanteur.

RIGHT/RECHTS/CI-CONTRE
PORTRAIT FOR 'ENTER MADAME' (1935)
Comically eager to escape the egoistic furies of an opera diva (Elissa Landi). / Auf komische Weise versucht er, sich den egoistischen Ausfällen einer Operndiva (Elissa Landi) zu entziehen. / Tentant désespérément d'échapper aux fureurs narcissiques d'une diva (Elissa Landi).

PAGES 48/49
ON THE SET OF 'WINGS IN THE DARK' (1935)
Grant invents instruments for 'flying blind', only to be blinded in an accident. / Ken Gordon (Grant) erfindet Instrumente für den ‚Blindflug' und verliert dann bei einem Unfall tatsächlich das Augenlicht. / Les instruments qu'il a inventés pour « voler à l'aveuglette » lui valent de se retrouver aveugle à la suite d'un accident.

PAGES 50/51
ADVERT FOR 'WINGS IN THE DARK' (1935)
Myrna Loy is the stunt-pilot who loves Grant, restoring his life if not his sight. / Myrna Loy spielt die Kunstfliegerin, die in Ken verliebt ist und ihm sein Selbstbewusstsein zurückgibt – wenn auch nicht seine Sehkraft. / Myrna Loy en pilote acrobatique amoureuse de Grant, qui va lui rendre la vie, sinon la vue.

NC

"WINGS IN

PARAMOUNT'S headline dramatic romance "WINGS
names, MYRNA LOY and Cary Grant with Roscoe Ka

"A box-office bulls-eye, and a piece of screen craftmanship in direction, playing, writing, technical assembly and presentation which is something to see and ponder and admire."
—*Hollywood Variety*

"A story so different in every phase it has no counterpart. 'Wings in the Dark' may prove one of the season's prize successes."
—*Motion Picture Herald*

"High above average. Fine entertainment for men and women. Its name values should send it soaring for real grosses."
—*Motion Picture Daily*

HE DARK"

THE DARK" starring two great box-office
Herbert Cavanaugh . . . . then comes . . . .

STILL FROM 'THE LAST OUTPOST' (1935)
Captive to a brilliant, half-mad officer modeled on T. E. Lawrence (Claude Rains). / Michael (Grant) ist einem genialen, halbverrückten Offizier (Claude Rains) ausgeliefert, der T. E. Lawrence nachempfunden ist. / Prisonnier d'un brillant officier à moitié fou (Claude Rains) inspiré de T. E. Lawrence.

"The only really good thing about acting is that there's no heavy lifting."
Cary Grant

„Das einzig wirklich Gute an der Schauspielerei ist, dass man dabei keine schweren Lasten heben muss."
Cary Grant

« La seule bonne chose dans le métier d'acteur, c'est qu'on n'a pas à soulever de lourdes charges. »
Cary Grant

STILL FROM 'THE LAST OUTPOST' (1935)
In love with the half-mad officer's bride, Gertrude Michael. / Obendrein ist Michael in die Verlobte (Gertrude Michael) des halbverrückten Offiziers verliebt. / Amoureux de la jeune épouse de l'officier à moitié fou, Gertrude Michael.

STILL FROM 'SYLVIA SCARLETT' (1935)
Clowning for the first time in a film opposite Katharine Hepburn (right). / Zum ersten Mal spielt er den Clown in einem Film neben Katharine Hepburn (rechts). / Cary Grant fait pour la première fois le pitre dans un film, aux côtés de Katharine Hepburn (à droite).

"He was comfortable in all aspects of show business: acrobatics, singing, music, comedy, drama, the circus..."
Gregory Peck

„Er fühlte sich in allen Bereichen des Showgeschäfts wohl: Akrobatik, Gesang, Musik, Komödie, Drama, Zirkus ..."
Gregory Peck

« Il était à l'aise dans toutes les disciplines du show business : acrobatie, chant, musique, comédie, tragédie, cirque... »
Gregory Peck

STILL FROM 'SYLVIA SCARLETT' (1935)
As his fellow fugitive, Hepburn memorably, and sexily, travels in drag. / Sylvia (Hepburn), wie Jimmy (Grant) auf der Flucht, verkleidet sich eindrucksvoll – und sehr sexy – als Junge. / Parmi ces trois fuyards se cache Katharine Hepburn, inoubliable en travesti.

STILL FROM 'THE AMAZING QUEST OF ERNEST BLISS' (1936)

As a once-spoiled millionaire sworn to earn his living for a year, consoled by Buena Bent. / Als ehemals verwöhnter Millionär, der wettet, dass er ein Jahr lang seinen Lebensunterhalt selbst verdienen kann, findet er Trost bei Mrs. Mott (Buena Bent). / En millionnaire ayant juré de gagner sa vie pendant un an, consolé ici par Buena Bent.

"It's important to know where you've come from so that you can know where you're going. I probably chose my profession because I was seeking approval, adulation, admiration and affection."
Cary Grant

„Es ist wichtig zu wissen, wo man herkommt, um zu wissen, wo man hin will. Ich habe vermutlich meinen Beruf gewählt, weil ich Anerkennung, Schmeichelei, Bewunderung und Zuneigung suchte."
Cary Grant

« Il est important de savoir d'où l'on vient pour savoir où l'on va. J'ai sans doute choisi ce métier parce que j'étais en quête de reconnaissance, d'adulation, d'admiration et d'affection. »
Cary Grant

STILL FROM 'BIG BROWN EYES' (1936)
With Joan Bennett (left) in a complicated thriller full of murders, traps and escapades. / Mit Joan Bennett (links) in einem komplexen Thriller voller Mord, Fallen und Eskapaden. / Avec Joan Bennett (à gauche) dans un thriller truffé de meurtres, de pièges et de rebondissements.

ON THE SET OF 'SUZY' (1936)
Between takes, filming Harlow and co-star Franchot Tone (center). / In einer Drehpause filmt er Harlow und seinen Kollegen Franchot Tone (Mitte). / Entre les prises, il s'amuse à filmer Jean Harlow et son partenaire Franchot Tone (au centre).

PORTRAIT FOR 'SUZY' (1936)
As a French aviator stealing the heart of Jean Harlow. / Als französischer Flieger stiehlt er das Herz von Suzy (Jean Harlow). / En aviateur français ravissant le cœur de Jean Harlow.

LOBBY CARD FOR 'WEDDING PRESENT' (1936)
He steals Joan Bennett from her wedding in an ambulance marked 'looney bin.' / Er entführt Rusty (Joan Bennett) von ihrer Hochzeit in einem Krankenwagen mit der Aufschrift „Irrenanstalt". / Il enlève Joan Bennett le jour de son mariage dans une ambulance portant l'inscription « Asile de fous ».

STILL FROM 'WHEN YOU'RE IN LOVE' (1937)
He and Grace Moore marry for convenience, but are soon stuck on each other. / Jimmy (Grant) und Louise (Grace Moore) gehen eine Zweckehe ein, sind aber bald darauf unzertrennlich. / Un mariage de raison avec Grace Moore qui tourne au mariage d'amour.

STILL FROM 'TOPPER' (1937)
As ghosts, Grant and Constance Bennett are only visible to Roland Young. / Als Geister sind Grant und Constance Bennett nur für Roland Young sichtbar. / Cary Grant et Constance Bennett en fantômes, visibles uniquement aux yeux de Roland Young.

"Actors today try to avoid comedy because if you write a comedy that's not a success, the lack of success is immediately apparent because the audience is not laughing. A comedy is a big risk."
Cary Grant

„Schauspieler gehen Komödien heutzutage lieber aus dem Weg. Wenn nämlich eine Komödie nicht funktioniert, merkt man es sofort, weil das Publikum nicht lacht. Eine Komödie ist immer ein großes Wagnis."
Cary Grant

« Aujourd'hui, les acteurs tentent d'éviter les comédies, car si une comédie n'a pas de succès, c'est immédiatement visible, puisque le public ne rit pas. La comédie, c'est très risqué. »
Cary Grant

STILL FROM 'TOPPER' (1937)
Having helped Topper to enjoy life, they melt happily into their hereafter. / Nachdem sie Topper die Freude am Leben zurückgegeben haben, können die beiden glücklich im Jenseits verschwinden. / Après avoir aidé Topper à profiter de la vie, ils disparaissent gaiement dans l'au-delà.

LOBBY CARD FOR 'THE TOAST OF NEW YORK' (1937)

In the 1860s, Grant helps a corrupt New York boss (Edward Arnold). / In den sechziger Jahren des 19. Jahrhunderts hilft Nick (Grant) einem korrupten New Yorker Unternehmer (Edward Arnold). / Complice d'un homme d'affaires corrompu (Edward Arnold) dans les années 1860.

RIGHT/RECHTS/CI-CONTRE

STILL FROM 'THE TOAST OF NEW YORK' (1937)

Jim Fisk (Edward Arnold) was a historic figure, Grant's character an invention. / Jim Fisk (Edward Arnold) basiert auf einer historischen Gestalt, während Grants Rolle frei erfunden ist. / Jim Fisk (Edward Arnold) est un personnage réel, tandis que celui de Grant est une pure invention.

PAGE 66

PORTRAIT FOR 'THE AWFUL TRUTH' (1937)

On a motorcycle with Irene Dunne, all the joys and perils of love in view. / Auf dem Motorrad fahren Jerry (Grant) und Lucy (Irene Dunne) den Freuden und Gefahren der Liebe entgegen. / À moto avec Irene Dunne, en route pour les plaisirs et les périls de l'amour.

A CIRCUS IN HIS HEAD

ZIRKUS IM KOPF
UNE ÂME DE CLOWN

"Irene Dunne's timing was marvelous. She was so good that she made comedy look easy. If she'd made it look as difficult as it really is, she would have won her Oscar."
Cary Grant

„Irene Dunnes Timing war wunderbar. Sie war so gut, dass Komik bei ihr wie ein Kinderspiel aussah. Hätte sie den Zuschauer ahnen lassen, wie schwierig das tatsächlich ist, hätte sie ihren Oscar gewonnen."
Cary Grant

« Irene Dunne avait un merveilleux sens du rythme. Elle était si douée qu'avec elle, jouer la comédie semblait facile. Si elle avait montré à quel point c'était difficile, elle aurait remporté un oscar. »
Cary Grant

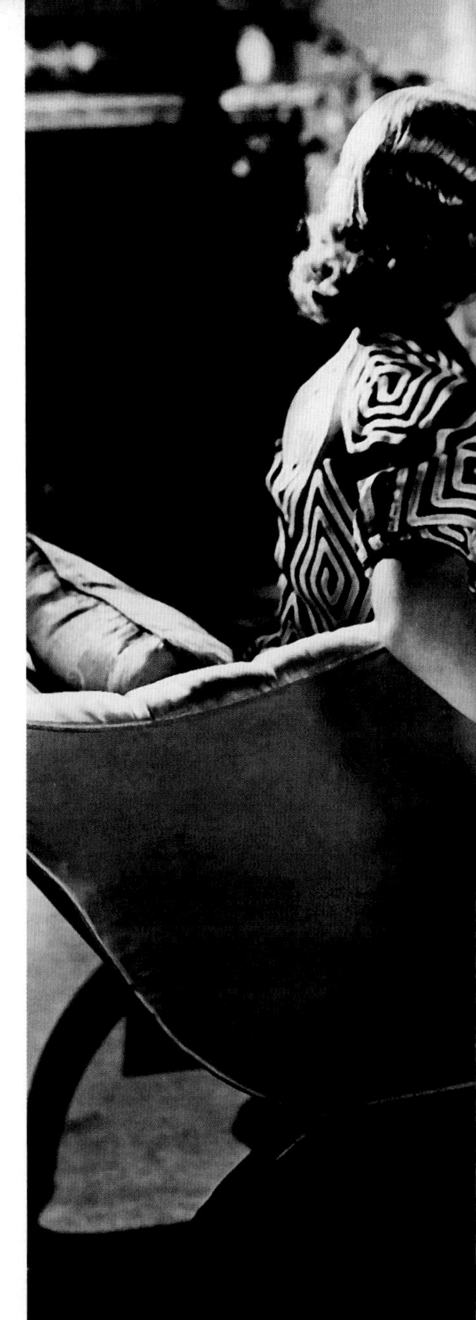

STILL FROM 'THE AWFUL TRUTH' (1937)
Dunne and Asta the Dog keep something from a philandering Cary. / Lucy (Dunne) und Asta der Hund haben etwas vor Schürzenjäger Jerry zu verbergen. / Irene Dunne et le chien Asta ont quelque chose à cacher au mari volage.

LOBBY CARD FOR 'BRINGING UP BABY' (1938)
Unappreciated in its day, now beloved for the sheer velocity of its madcap farce. / Zu seiner Zeit wurde der Film nicht besonders beachtet, aber heute ist er schon allein wegen seiner temporeichen und turbulenten Komik beliebt. / Une farce excentrique plutôt mal reçue à l'époque, mais aujourd'hui appréciée pour son rythme décoiffant.

STILL FROM 'BRINGING UP BABY' (1938)
Telling off Hepburn, a daffy, angelic troublemaker deaf to all reason. / David (Grant) liest Susan (Katharine Hepburn) die Leviten, doch vernünftige Argumente stoßen bei dieser ebenso verrückten wie engelhaften Unruhestifterin auf taube Ohren. / Grant sermonne Hepburn, semeuse de troubles angélique et loufoque.

STILL FROM 'HOLIDAY' (1938)
Charming Hepburn atop her own childhood toy. / Auf ihrem Dreirad aus Kindertagen lässt Johnny (Grant) bei Linda (Katharine Hepburn) seinen Charme spielen. / Grant enfourche le vieux tricycle de Katharine Hepburn, qui succombe à son charme.

STILL FROM 'HOLIDAY' (1938)
Cary proposed to Hepburn's sister, but Cupid has other plans. / Eigentlich ist Johnny mit Lindas Schwester verlobt, doch Amor hat andere Pläne. / C'est à la sœur de Katharine que Cary a demandé sa main, mais Cupidon ne l'entend pas de cette oreille.

STILL FROM 'IN NAME ONLY' (1939)
Collapsed with pneumonia as Carole Lombard, kneeling, attends to him. / Als Alec (Grant) mit einer Lungenentzündung zusammenbricht, kümmert sich Julie (Carole Lombard, kniend) um ihn. / Terrassé par une pneumonie tandis que Carole Lombard, à genoux, veille sur lui.

"Divorce is a game played by lawyers."
Cary Grant

„Scheidung ist ein Spiel, das Rechtsanwälte spielen."
Cary Grant

« Le divorce est un jeu entre avocats. »
Cary Grant

STILL FROM 'IN NAME ONLY' (1939)
In a loveless marriage with Kay Francis, despite his love for Lombard. / Alec steckt in einer lieblosen Ehe mit Maida (Kay Francis, rechts), liebt aber Julie. / Marié à Kay Francis (à droite), malgré son amour pour Carole Lombard.

STILL FROM 'GUNGA DIN' (1939)
At the mercy of pals Victor McLaglen, Douglas Fairbanks, Jr., and a turbaned Sam Jaffe. / Cutter (Grant) ist seinen Kameraden Mac (Victor McLaglen) und Tommy (Douglas Fairbanks, Jr.) sowie dem Wasserträger Gunga Din (Sam Jaffe, mit Turban) ausgeliefert. / À la merci de ses compères Victor McLaglen et Douglas Fairbanks Jr., avec un Sam Jaffe enturbanné.

PORTRAIT FOR 'GUNGA DIN' (1939)
A romantic figure in love with rollicking adventure, directed by the great George Stevens. / Eine romantische Figur, die das große Abenteuer liebt – unter der Regie des großartigen George Stevens. / Un personnage romantique passionné d'aventure et de rigolade, mis en scène par le grand George Stevens.

STILL FROM 'ONLY ANGELS HAVE WINGS' (1939)

Running an airfield in South America, and homing in on Jean Arthur. / Als Chef einer Gruppe von Postfliegern in Südamerika probt Grant hier den Anflug auf Bonnie (Jean Arthur). / Aviateur dans une compagnie aéropostale en Amérique du Sud, Grant effectue un piqué sur Jean Arthur.

"To succeed with the opposite sex, tell her you are impotent. She can't wait to disprove it."
Cary Grant

„Um beim anderen Geschlecht Erfolg zu haben, muss man der Frau erzählen, man sei impotent. Dann kann sie es gar nicht abwarten, das Gegenteil zu beweisen."
Cary Grant

« Pour avoir du succès auprès des dames, dites-leur que vous êtes impuissant. Elles n'auront de cesse de vous prouver le contraire. »
Cary Grant

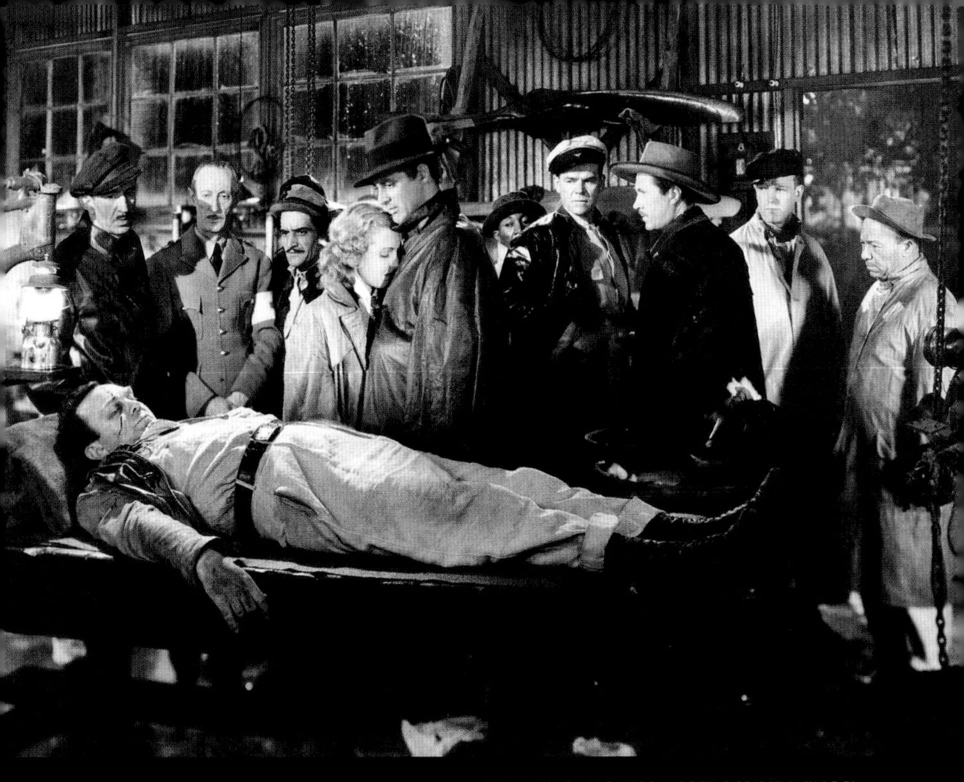

STILL FROM 'ONLY ANGELS HAVE WINGS' (1939)

Airmen stoically comfort their dying colleague (Thomas Mitchell). / Die Fliegertruppe tröstet einen sterbenden Kameraden (Thomas Mitchell). / Les aviateurs réconfortent avec stoïcisme leur collègue mortellement blessé (Thomas Mitchell).

STILL FROM 'HIS GIRL FRIDAY' (1940)
With Rosalind Russell. He's a top newspaper editor, she's his ace reporter. / Mit Rosalind Russell. Er spielt den Chefredakteur einer großen Zeitung, sie seine beste Reporterin. / Avec Rosalind Russell, reporter de choc dans le journal dont il est rédacteur en chef.

"Most women are instinctively wiser and emotionally more mature than men. They know our insecurities. A man rushes about trying to prove himself. It takes him much longer to feel comfortable about getting married."
Cary Grant

„Die meisten Frauen sind instinktiv weiser und emotional reifer als Männer. Sie kennen unsere Unsicherheiten. Ein Mann stürzt hierhin und dorthin, um sich zu beweisen. Er braucht viel länger, um sich mit dem Gedanken an die Ehe anzufreunden."
Cary Grant

STILL FROM 'HIS GIRL FRIDAY' (1940)
They were married to each other, once, but the divorce just hasn't worked out. / Sie waren einmal verheiratet – die Scheidung haben sie aber noch nicht verwunden. / Un couple désuni qui ne s'est pas remis de sa séparation.

« La plupart des femmes sont instinctivement plus sages et émotionnellement plus mûres que les hommes. Elles connaissent nos angoisses. Un homme s'agite pour tenter de faire ses preuves. Il lui faut beaucoup plus de temps pour s'habituer à l'idée du mariage. »
Cary Grant

STILL FROM 'MY FAVORITE WIFE' (1940)
Dunne is being wooed by Randolph Scott, but Grant still loves her. / Auch wenn Ellen (Dunne) von Stephen (Randolph Scott) umworben wird, liebt Nick (Grant) sie nach wie vor. / Bien qu'Irene Dunne se fasse courtiser par Randolph Scott, Cary Grant l'aime toujours.

PORTRAIT FOR 'MY FAVORITE WIFE' (1940)
Thought lost at sea, ex-wife Irene Dunne survived on an island, and has come back. / Die auf See verschollen geglaubte Ex-Frau (Irene Dunne) überlebte auf einer Insel und ist zurückgekehrt. / Perdue en mer, son ex-femme (Irene Dunne) a survécu sur une île et réapparaît un beau jour.

STILL FROM 'THE HOWARDS OF VIRGINIA' (1940)

With Martha Scott. Generally, Grant was poorly suited to costume pieces. / Mit Martha Scott. Allgemein standen Grant historische Stoffe nicht gut zu Gesicht. / Cary Grant, ici avec Martha Scott, n'est guère dans son élément dans les films historiques.

PORTRAIT FOR 'THE HOWARDS OF VIRGINIA' (1940)

Weary after long battles with the British army, circa 1776. / Müde von der langen Schlacht gegen die Briten – um 1776. / Las des longues batailles contre l'armée britannique, vers 1776.

STILL FROM 'THE PHILADELPHIA STORY' (1940)
Grant and James Stewart compete comically for Hepburn's affections. / Dexter (Grant) und Macauley (James Stewart) liefern sich einen komischen Konkurrenzkampf um die Gunst von Tracy Lord (Hepburn). / Cary Grant et James Stewart en rivaux cocasses tentant de gagner les faveurs de Katharine Hepburn.

ON THE SET OF 'THE PHILADELPHIA STORY' (1940)
Katharine Hepburn executive-produced this gem to revitalize her career, and succeeded. / Um ihrer Karriere neuen Schwung zu verleihen, war Katharine Hepburn bei diesem Filmjuwel auch ausführende Produzentin – mit großem Erfolg. / Un petit bijou destiné à relancer la carrière de Katharine Hepburn, qui en est le producteur exécutif.

STILL FROM 'PENNY SERENADE' (1941)
Meeting Irene Dunne, at the sweet start of their often tragic marriage. / Roger (Grant) trifft Julie (Irene Dunne) am Anfang ihrer oftmals tragischen Beziehung. / Rencontre avec Irene Dunne, prémices d'un mariage émaillé de drames.

STILL FROM 'PENNY SERENADE' (1941)
Having suffered the death of one child, they adopt another. / Nach dem Tod eines Kindes adoptieren sie ein zweites. / Après la mort de leur enfant, ils décident d'en adopter un autre.

PAGE 90
PORTRAIT FOR 'NOTORIOUS' (1946)

SHADY

SCHATTENSPIEL

UNE PART D'OMBRE

STILL FROM 'SUSPICION' (1941)
Cast brilliantly against type as a possibly lethal seducer, opposite Joan Fontaine. / Eine genial untypische Besetzung für Grant in der Rolle eines möglicherweise mörderischen Verführers an der Seite von Joan Fontaine. / Délicieusement à contre-emploi en séducteur soupçonné de penchants meurtriers par sa partenaire Joan Fontaine.

ADVERT FOR 'SUSPICION' (1941)
Part of Grant's enduring magnetism is the subtle aura of danger under the charm. / Einen Teil seiner unvergänglichen Anziehungskraft verdankt Grant der unterschwelligen Gefährlichkeit hinter seiner charmanten Ausstrahlung. / Le charisme de Cary Grant découle aussi de la part d'ombre que l'on devine sous son charme.

CARY GRANT

in

"BEFORE THE FACT"

An action-murder-romance novel to be directed by the master of thrills and melodrama—

ALFRED HITCHCOCK

Harry E. Edington, Executive Producer

MEMO

✓ They Knew What They Wanted
✓ Too Many Girls
✓ You'll Find Out
✓ Little Men
✓ Kitty Foyle
✓ No, No, Nanette
✓ Citizen Kane
✓ Mr. and Mrs. Smith
✓ The Devil and Miss Jones
✓ Before The Fact

STILL FROM 'SUSPICION' (1941)
Hurtling toward the climax. Is he a killer or not? Hitchcock filmed it both ways. / Die Handlung rast ihrem Höhepunkt zu: Ist er ein Mörder oder nicht? Hitchcock drehte beide Versionen. / Assassin ou innocent ? Hitchcock a tourné deux versions du dénouement.

PAGES 96/97
STILL FROM 'THE TALK OF THE TOWN' (1942)
Grant is a political radical wrongly accused of murder. / Grant spielt einen Radikalen, der zu Unrecht eines Mordes bezichtigt wird. / En militant politique accusé à tort de meurtre.

STILL FROM 'SUSPICION' (1941)
Director Alfred Hitchcock fitted a special light in that milk, to give it a sinister glow. / Regisseur Alfred Hitchcock versteckte eine spezielle Lampe im Milchglas, um es besonders unheimlich wirken zu lassen. / Alfred Hitchcock a installé un dispositif lumineux dans le verre de lait pour qu'il brille d'une lueur inquiétante.

PAGES 98/99
STILL FROM 'ONCE UPON A HONEYMOON' (1942)
With Ginger Rogers, navigating an odd mix of comedy and wartime romance. / Mit Ginger Rogers in einer kuriosen Mischung aus Komödie und Kriegsromanze. / Avec Ginger Rogers dans un étrange mélange de comédie et de romantisme sur fond de guerre.

HOTEL
MARSZAŁKA

HOTEL

STILL FROM 'MR. LUCKY' (1943)
Grant assumes a dead man's identity, only to take on that man's problems. / Joe (Grant) nimmt die Identität eines Toten an, lädt sich damit aber auch dessen Probleme auf. / En usurpant l'identité d'un mort, Grant hérite également de ses problèmes.

PAGES 102/103
ADVERT FOR 'DESTINATION TOKYO' (1943)
Commanding a submarine in this first-rate wartime melodrama. / In diesem erstklassigen Kriegsmelodram spielt er den Kommandanten eines U-Boots. / Aux commandes d'un sous-marin dans un excellent mélodrame tourné pendant la guerre.

PAGES 104/105
ADVERTS FOR 'ONCE UPON A TIME' (1944)
Grant plays a shady producer enamored of a dancing caterpillar. / Grant spielt einen zwielichtigen Produzenten, der Gefallen an einer tanzenden Raupe findet. / En producteur véreux captivé par une chenille dansante.

STILL FROM 'MR. LUCKY' (1943)
A moody embrace in the cold mist, with Laraine Day. / Eine stimmungsvolle Umarmung im kalten Nebel, mit Laraine Day. / Étreinte avec Laraine Day dans l'atmosphère funeste d'une brume glacée.

Support the Fourth War Loan!

COVER THE ENTIRE
EXHIBITION FIELD
AND AGAIN YOU
WILL FIND THAT
THE BIGGEST
PICTURE IS A
WARNER BROS.
PICTURE!

CARY GRANT
AND
JOHN GARFIELD
IN
"DESTINATION
TOKYO"

with DANE CLARK · ROBERT HUTTON · WARNER ANDERSON
ALAN HALE · JOHN RIDGELY · WILLIAM PRINCE
Directed by DELMER DAVES · Produced by JERRY WALD
Screen Play by Delmer Daves and Albert Maltz · From an Original Story by Steve Fisher · Music by Franz Waxman

Once upon a time . . . .

This is the Fabulous Story of a Fabulous Guy

... and the wonderful things that happen to him ... and to YOU! A timeless tale of today... whimsically woven of romance ... and tenderness... laughter ... and that thing called "heart".

"I've often been accused by critics of being myself onscreen. But being oneself is more difficult than you'd suppose."
Cary Grant

„Kritiker haben mir oft vorgeworfen, ich spielte auf der Leinwand nur mich selbst. Aber man selbst zu sein ist viel schwieriger, als man denkt."
Cary Grant

« J'ai souvent été accusé par les critiques d'être moi-même à l'écran. Mais être soi-même est plus difficile qu'il n'y paraît. »
Cary Grant

PAGES 108/109
STILL FROM 'NONE BUT THE LONELY HEART' (1944)
The most passionately undertaken role of Grant's career. / Von allen Rollen seiner Karriere spielte Grant diese mit der größten Leidenschaft. / Le rôle dans lequel il s'est investi le plus personnellement.

ADVERT FOR 'NONE BUT THE LONELY HEART' (1944)
Adapted and directed by Clifford Odets from the novel by Richard Llewellyn. / Richard Llewellyns Roman wurde von Clifford Odets adaptiert, der auch Regie führte. / Adapté et réalisé par Clifford Odets, d'après le roman de Richard Llewellyn.

ME?

I'm Ernie Mott...
I make my own
rules for life
and love!"

Boy, watch the femmes go for this!

STILL FROM 'NONE BUT THE LONELY HEART' (1944)
Grant's pain-filled relationship with his actual mother informed this one with Ethel Barrymore. / Grant ließ das schmerzvolle Verhältnis zu seiner eigenen Mutter in die Beziehung seiner Figur zu ihrer Mutter (Ethel Barrymore) einfließen. / Les relations douloureuses de Cary Grant avec sa propre mère influencent son jeu aux côtés d'Ethel Barrymore.

STILL FROM 'NONE BUT THE LONELY HEART' (1944)
Loitering with Barry Fitzgerald. This raw London underworld might have been Grant's real-life fate. / Ernie (Grant) und Henry (Barry Fitzgerald) lungern in dunklen Gassen: Diese rohe Londoner Unterwelt hätte durchaus Grants eigenes Schicksal sein können. / En vadrouille avec Barry Fitzgerald. Le destin de Cary Grant aurait pu le mener dans ces bas-fonds londoniens dans la vraie vie.

MARY
1847·1881

STILL FROM 'ARSENIC AND OLD LACE' (1944)
Between Raymond Massey and Peter Lorre, Grant is the sane oddball in a farcical household. / Zwischen Raymond Massey und Peter Lorre spielt Grant den einzig „Normalen" in einem völlig ausgeflippten Haus. / Entre Raymond Massey et Peter Lorre, Grant est le seul esprit sain dans une maison de fous.

STILL FROM 'ARSENIC AND OLD LACE' (1944)
"But, Mortimer, you're going to love me for my mind, too?" pleads Priscilla Lane. Grant quips: "One thing at a time." / „Aber du liebst mich doch auch wegen meines Verstandes?", fragt Elaine (Priscilla Lane). Mortimer (Grant) antwortet: „Eins nach dem anderen." / « Mais, Mortimer, vous m'aimez aussi pour mon esprit, n'est-ce-pas ? », implore Priscilla Lane. « Chaque chose en son temps », rétorque Cary Grant.

STILL FROM 'NIGHT AND DAY' (1946)
A biography of songwriter Cole Porter (Grant), co-starring Jane Wyman and Monte Woolley. / Eine Biographie des Liederkomponisten Cole Porter (Grant), mit Jane Wyman und Monte Woolley in weiteren Hauptrollen. / Une biographie de l'auteur-compositeur Cole Porter (Grant), avec Jane Wyman et Monte Woolley.

STILL FROM 'NIGHT AND DAY' (1946)
Alexis Smith, as Mrs. Cole Porter, coping with his war-wounds and horseback injuries. / Alexis Smith muss als Ehefrau Linda Lee Porter mit den Kriegs- und Reitverletzungen ihres Mannes zurechtkommen. / La femme de Cole Porter (Alexis Smith) l'aide à surmonter les séquelles de ses blessures de guerre et d'un grave accident de cheval.

"My formula for living is quite simple. I get up in the morning and I go to bed at night. In between, I occupy myself as best I can."
Cary Grant

„Meine Lebensformel ist recht einfach. Ich stehe morgens auf und gehe abends zu Bett. Dazwischen beschäftige ich mich, so gut ich kann."
Cary Grant

« Mon secret dans la vie, c'est bien simple. Je me lève le matin et je me couche le soir. Entre-temps, je m'occupe du mieux que je peux. »
Cary Grant

PORTRAIT FOR 'NOTORIOUS' (1946)
Alfred Hitchcock outwitted the censors' limits on kissing by weaving in cheek-to-cheek intensity. / Alfred Hitchcock umging die Auflagen der Zensur für die Dauer eines einzelnen Kusses, indem er ein paar Schmuseeinheiten einfügte. / Alfred Hitchcock déjoue la censure en remplaçant les baisers par d'ardentes étreintes joue contre joue.

"One doesn't direct the marvelous Cary Grant; one simply puts him in front of a camera and lets the audience identify with him."
Alfred Hitchcock

„Dem fabelhaften Cary Grant gibt man keine Regieanweisungen. Man stellt ihn einfach vor die Kamera und überlässt es dem Publikum, sich mit ihm zu identifizieren."
Alfred Hitchcock

« On ne dirige pas Cary Grant ; on le met devant la caméra et on laisse le public s'identifier à lui. »
Alfred Hitchcock

STILL FROM 'NOTORIOUS' (1946)
Ingrid Bergman, unhappily married to Claude Rains, miserably in love with fellow spy Grant. / Alicia (Ingrid Bergman) ist unglücklich mit Sebastian Huberman (Claude Rains) verheiratet und ebenso unglücklich in ihren Spionagekollegen Devlin (Grant) verliebt. / Ingrid Bergman, mariée par devoir à Claude Rains, est secrètement amoureuse d'un autre espion, Devlin (Cary Grant).

"The essence of his quality can be put quite simply: he can be attractive and unattractive simultaneously; there is a light and dark side to him, but, whichever is dominant, the other creeps into view."
David Thomson

„Man kann seine Qualitäten sehr einfach zusammenfassen: Er kann gleichzeitig attraktiv und unattraktiv sein; er besitzt eine helle und eine dunkle Seite, wobei die weniger dominante immer durchschimmert."
David Thomson

« Ce qui le distingue, c'est qu'il peut être attirant et repoussant à la fois. Il possède un côté clair et un côté obscur, mais quel que soit celui qui domine, l'autre n'est jamais loin. »
David Thomson

STILL FROM 'NOTORIOUS' (1946)
In loving Bergman, Grant's secret agent must repeatedly pretend to be cruel. / Aus Liebe zu Alicia muss Geheimagent Devlin mehrfach Brutalität vortäuschen. / Malgré son amour pour Ingrid Bergman, l'agent secret doit fréquemment faire mine d'être cruel.

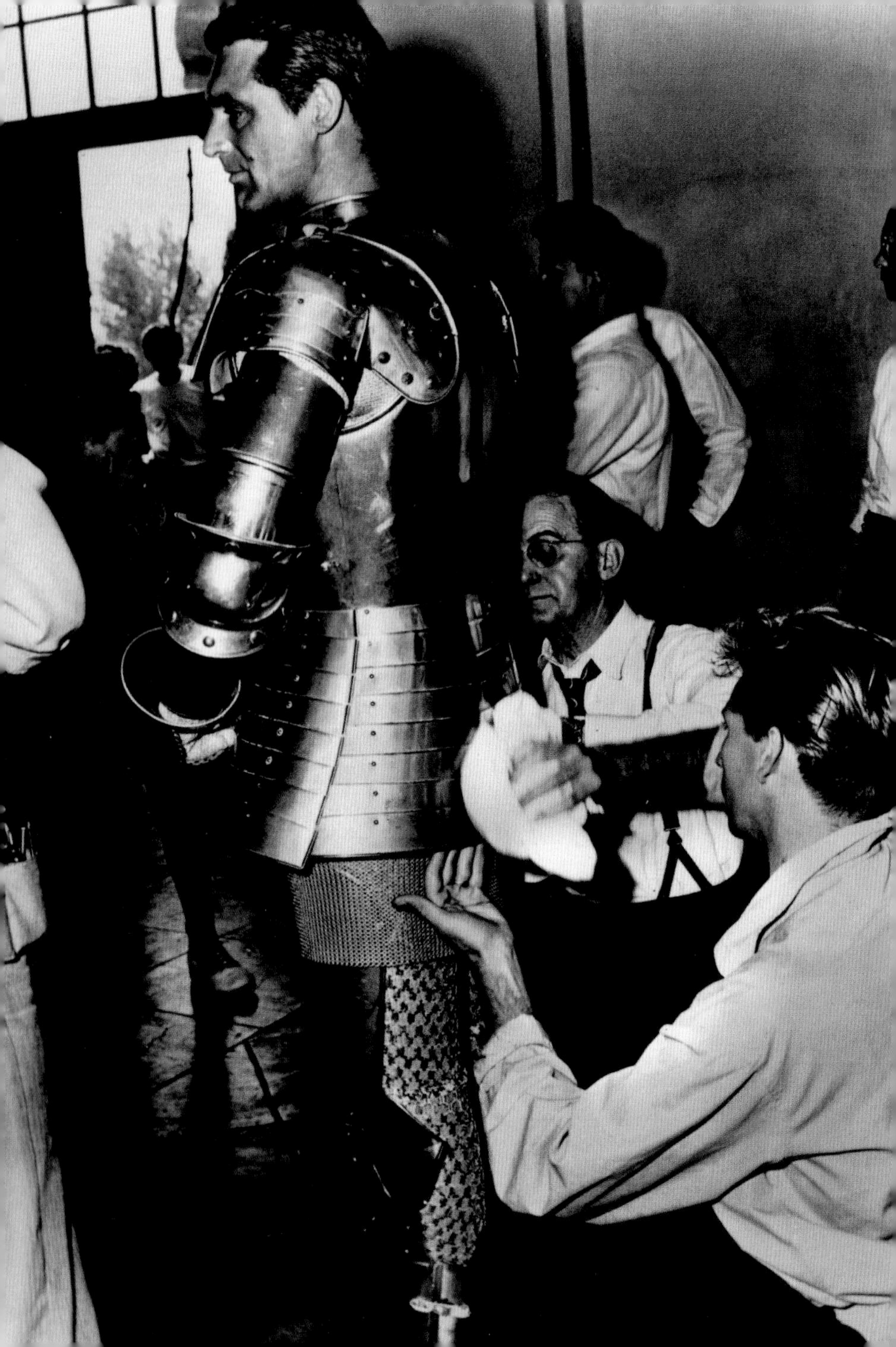

STILL FROM 'THE BACHELOR AND THE BOBBY-SOXER' (1947)
Shirley Temple (left) idolizes Grant, and he tries to guide her to boys her own age. / Susan (Shirley Temple, links) vergöttert Richard (Grant), während dieser versucht, ihr Interesse für Gleichaltrige zu wecken. / Idolâtré par Shirley Temple (à gauche), Grant tente de la détourner vers des garçons de son âge.

ON THE SET OF 'THE BACHELOR AND THE BOBBY-SOXER' (1947)
Literally 'a knight in shining armour' in the starry eyes of a female admirer. / In den verklärten Augen einer jungen Verehrerin wird Grant buchstäblich zum ‚Ritter in strahlender Rüstung'. / Littéralement transformé en « chevalier rutilant » dans les yeux enamourés d'une admiratrice.

STILL FROM 'THE BISHOP'S WIFE' (1947)
An explicitly angelic role, as he helps David Niven to better love Loretta Young. / Als Engel hilft Grant dem Bischof (David Niven), sich wieder mehr um seine vernachlässigte Frau (Loretta Young) zu kümmern. / Un rôle explicitement angélique, puisqu'il aide David Niven à mieux aimer Loretta Young.

STILL FROM 'MR. BLANDINGS BUILDS HIS DREAM HOUSE' (1948)
Standing off-kilter himself, after he's bought a 170-year-old house at 5 times its value. / Blandings verliert allmählich Halt und (Ver-)Stand, nachdem er ein 170 Jahre altes Haus zum Fünffachen seines Werts gekauft hat. / Légèrement déphasé, Blandings paye 5 fois son prix une bicoque délabrée vieille de 170 ans.

STILL FROM 'EVERY GIRL SHOULD BE MARRIED' (1948)
Cocking an ear in tandem with Drake, to hear what's being whispered. / Brown stellt die Lauscher auf, um mitzuhören, was Anabel ins Ohr geflüstert wird. / Tendant une oreille attentive aux messes basses du voisin de Betsy Drake.

PORTRAIT FOR 'EVERY GIRL SHOULD BE MARRIED' (1948)
Betsy Drake (above) has set her cap for him, and stalks him like a detective. / Anabel (Betsy Drake, oben) hat Dr. Brown (Grant) im Visier und stellt ihm wie ein Detektiv nach. / Bien décidée à l'épouser, Betsy Drake l'épie dans ses moindres mouvements.

STILL FROM 'I WAS A MALE WAR BRIDE' (1949)
This gallant French flyer will stop at nothing to be with his American wife (Ann Sheridan). / Dieser stattliche französische Flieger lässt nichts unversucht, um seine amerikanische Ehefrau (Ann Sheridan) wiederzusehen. / Ce galant aviateur français est prêt à tout pour rejoindre son épouse américaine (Ann Sheridan).

STILL FROM 'I WAS A MALE WAR BRIDE' (1949)
Sheridan can only bring Grant home as a "war bride" – hence, he cross-dresses. / Der französische Gemahl kann nur als „Kriegsbraut" in die USA einwandern – und so schlüpft er kurzerhand in Frauenkleider. / Ne pouvant entrer aux États-Unis que comme « épouse » d'un soldat américain, Cary Grant en est réduit à se travestir.

STILL FROM 'CRISIS' (1950)
As a surgeon held hostage by José Ferrer, a South American dictator suffering a tumor. / Als Chirurg wird Grant von einem tumorkranken südamerikanischen Diktator (José Ferrer) als Geisel festgehalten. / En chirurgien pris en otage par un dictateur sud-américain (José Ferrer) atteint d'une tumeur au cerveau.

"Some men squeeze a line to death. Cary tickles it into life."
Michael Curtiz

„Manche Leute quetschen einen Text zu Tode. Cary kitzelt ihn, bis er zum Leben erwacht."
Michael Curtiz

« Certains forcent leurs répliques jusqu'à les massacrer. Cary les titille jusqu'à ce qu'elles prennent vie. »
Michael Curtiz

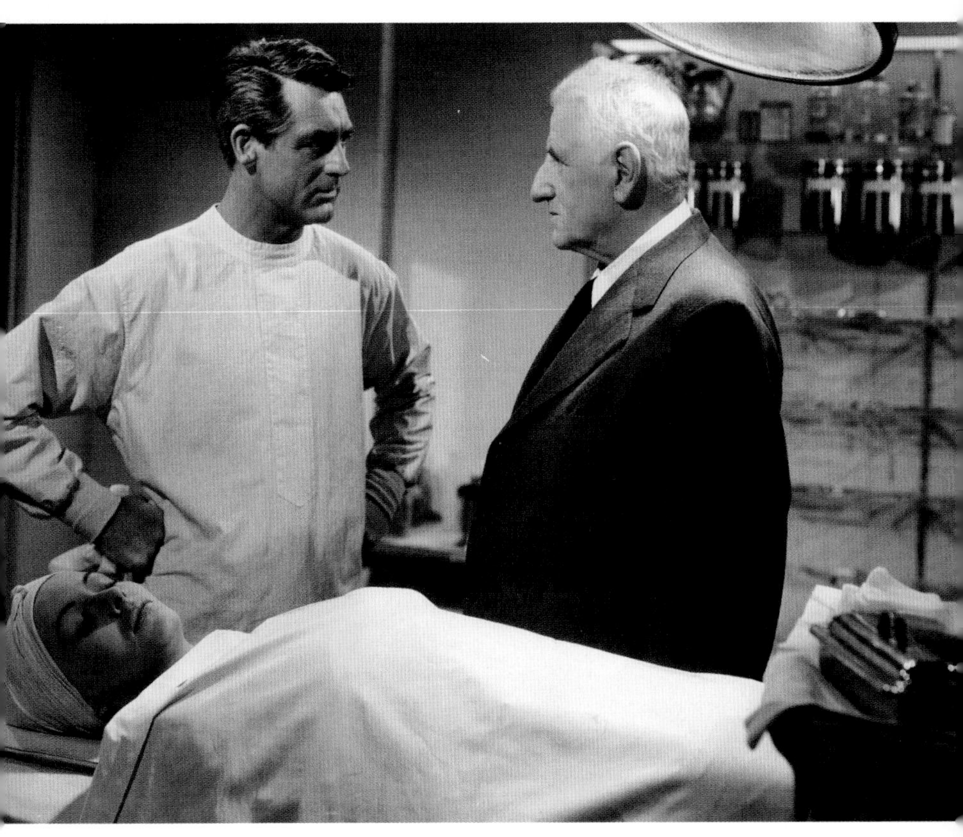

STILL FROM 'PEOPLE WILL TALK' (1951)
A persecuted professor of medicine, defending needed surgery for Jeanne Crain. / Als Medizinprofessor, der von Kollegen schikaniert wird, setzt sich Grant für eine notwendige Operation an Deborah (Jeanne Crain) ein. / En professeur de médecine persécuté, tentant de justifier l'opération de Jeanne Crain.

STILL FROM 'ROOM FOR ONE MORE' (1952)
Grant and Drake were a couple in real life into the early 1960s. / Bis Anfang der sechziger Jahre waren Grant und Drake auch privat ein Paar. / Cary Grant et Betsy Drake sont mariés dans la vraie vie jusqu'au début des années 1960.

STILL FROM 'ROOM FOR ONE MORE' (1952)
Chagrined that his kind wife (Betsy Drake, left) has opened their home to stray pets and children. / Poppy (Grant) ärgert es, dass seine gutmütige Frau (Betsy Drake, links) immer mehr streunende Tiere und Kinder zu Hause aufnimmt. / Chagriné que sa femme (Betsy Drake, à gauche) ouvre leur maison à une foule d'enfants et d'animaux abandonnés.

15

STILL FROM 'DREAM WIFE' (1953)
As an oil executive who thinks he wants a submissive Middle-Eastern bride, but Deborah Kerr has other plans. / Als Ölmagnat glaubt Grant, er müsse sich eine unterwürfige Braut aus dem Nahen Osten (Betta St. John) zulegen. Aber Deborah Kern hat andere Pläne. / En magnat du pétrole rêvant d'une épouse soumise venue d'Orient (Betta St. John).

PAGE 134
STILL FROM 'TO CATCH A THIEF' (1955)

STILL FROM 'MONKEY BUSINESS' (1952)
Inventor of a youth serum, manfully resisting the charms of Marilyn Monroe. / Als Erfinder eines Verjüngungstrunks widersetzt sich Grant mannhaft den Reizen von Marilyn Monroe. / Inventeur d'un sérum de jouvence, Grant résiste vaillamment aux charmes de Marilyn Monroe.

WACHSTUM

L’ABOUTISSEMENT

STILL FROM 'TO CATCH A THIEF' (1955)
Intoxicating romance opposite Grace Kelly, on the French Riviera. / Eine berauschende Romanze an der französischen Riviera, mit Grace Kelly. / Une envoûtante histoire d'amour avec Grace Kelly, sous le soleil de la côte d'Azur.

"I have spent the greater part of my life fluctuating between Archie Leach and Cary Grant, unsure of each, suspecting each."
Cary Grant

„Ich habe den größten Teil meines Lebens damit verbracht, zwischen Archie Leach und Cary Grant hin- und herzupendeln. Bei keinem fühlte ich mich sicher, beiden misstraute ich."
Cary Grant

« J'ai passé la majeure partie de ma vie à osciller entre Archie Leach et Cary Grant en doutant de l'un comme de l'autre, en ne me fiant à aucun des deux. »
Cary Grant

STILL FROM 'TO CATCH A THIEF' (1955)
A former jewel thief, reformed after service in the French resistance, framed by a clever copycat. / Ein ehemaliger Juwelendieb, der nach seiner Beteiligung am französischen Widerstand auf den rechten Weg zurückgefunden hat, wird von einem gerissenen Nachahmer hereingelegt. / Ancien cambrioleur assagi depuis la Résistance, il est soupçonné à cause d'un faussaire qui imite ses méthodes.

STILL FROM 'TO CATCH A THIEF' (1955)
As always, director Hitchcock makes brilliant use of the sexy dualities in Grant's nature. / Wie immer versteht Regisseur Hitchcock die erotisch reizvolle Zwiespältigkeit im Wesen Grants geschickt einzusetzen. / Comme toujours, Hitchcock exploite à merveille l'attirante dualité de l'acteur.

"The most publicly seduced male the world has known."
Pauline Kael

„Der am öffentlichsten verführte Mann, den die Welt je kannte."
Pauline Kael

« L'homme le plus publiquement convoité qui ait jamais existé. »
Pauline Kael

STILL FROM 'TO CATCH A THIEF' (1955)
The fireworks are about to begin. Grace Kelly reveals a sexy duality of her own. / Kurz vor dem Feuerwerk enthüllt Frances (Grace Kelly) reizvoll ihre eigene erotische Zwiespältigkeit. / Alors que le feu d'artifice va commencer, Grace Kelly révèle une dualité non moins attirante.

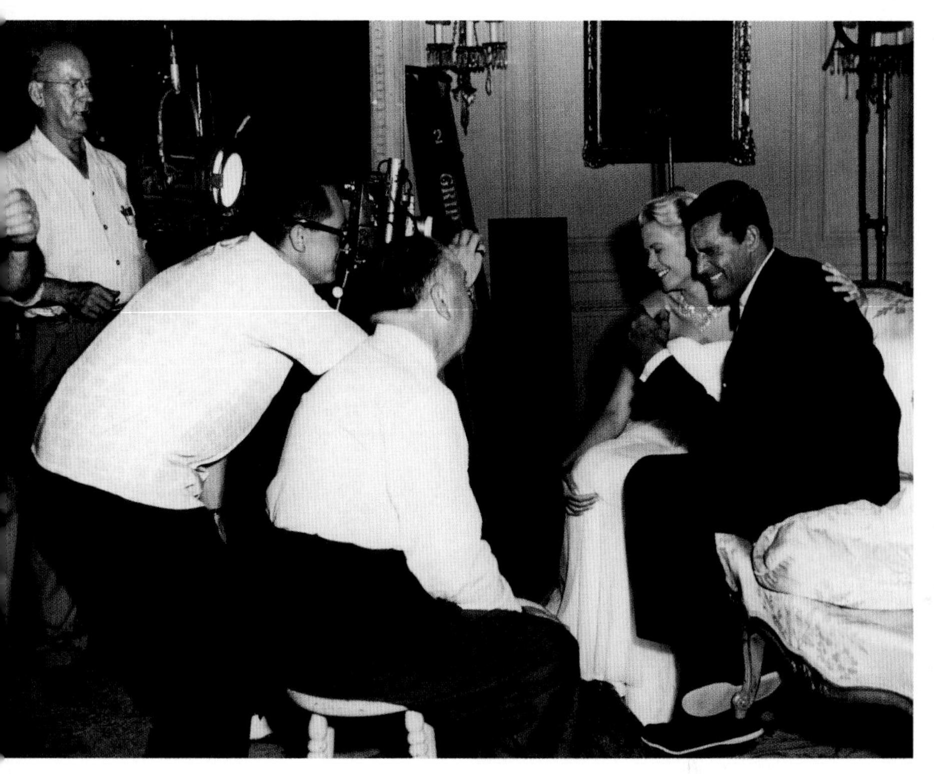

ON THE SET OF 'TO CATCH A THIEF' (1955)
Hitchcock (left), ever ready with a quip, relaxes his two lead actors. / Hitchcock (links), immer zu Späßen aufgelegt, lockert seine beiden Hauptdarsteller auf. / Hitchcock (à gauche) a toujours le bon mot pour détendre ses acteurs.

STILL FROM 'TO CATCH A THIEF' (1955)
Such passionate chemistry merited sequels, but Kelly married and became Grace of Monaco. / Eine derartige Leidenschaft hätte eine Fortsetzung verdient, doch Kelly heiratete und wurde zur Fürstin von Monaco. / Une si parfaite alchimie laissait espérer d'autres films, mais Grace Kelly se marie et devient Grace de Monaco.

STILL FROM 'TO CATCH A THIEF' (1955)
If he is to clear his name, our hero must risk becoming like a burglar to trap his foe. / Um seine Unschuld beweisen zu können, muss John (Grant) wieder den Einbrecher mimen, bis sein Gegenspieler in die Falle tappt. / Afin de se disculper, notre héros doit lui-même agir comme un cambrioleur pour démasquer l'usurpateur.

ON THE SET OF 'TO CATCH A THIEF' (1955)
Hitchcock's crew films this climactic sequence. / Hitchcocks Crew beim Dreh dieses spannenden Filmhöhepunkts. / L'équipe de Hitchcock pendant le tournage de la séquence décisive.

STILL FROM 'AN AFFAIR TO REMEMBER' (1957)

A cherished classic of Grant's later career, co-starring Deborah Kerr, directed by Leo McCarey. / Ein kostbares Kleinod aus Grants Spätwerk, unter der Regie von Leo McCarey mit Deborah Kerr in der weiblichen Hauptrolle. / L'un des classiques de la fin de sa carrière, tourné avec Deborah Kerr sous la direction de Leo McCarey.

STILL FROM 'AN AFFAIR TO REMEMBER' (1957)

Both are crossing the ocean toward other loves, but their affair here alters their lives. / Beide überqueren den Ozean auf dem Weg zu ihren jeweiligen Verlobten, doch ihre Begegnung an Bord des Schiffes gibt ihrem Schicksal eine Wende. / Tous deux traversent l'océan pour rejoindre l'élu de leur cœur, mais leur rencontre va changer le cours de leur vie.

Scene from 20th Century-Fox's production of Leo McCarey's **"AN AFFAIR TO REMEMBER,"** co-starring **CARY GRANT** and **DEBORAH KERR**, which takes place aboard the s.s. *Constitution*. A Jerry Wald Production in CinemaScope. Color by Deluxe.

A Voyage to Remember

A Sunlane Cruise to Europe this Fall or Winter can be *your* voyage to remember. For as little as $535 in Cabin Class or $685 in First, you can sail aboard the great *Independence* or *Constitution* for a luxurious 3-week round trip to the Mediterranean!

The *Independence* and *Constitution* will be sailing from New York approximately every two weeks all this Fall and early Winter through January. You'll have time to visit ashore at 3 to 8 ports, such as *Canary Islands, Casablanca, Barcelona, Cannes, Genoa, Naples, Tangier, Madeira.*

At sea there's fun, glamour, relaxation! And you'll have an air conditioned stateroom, private bathroom with shower, enjoy absolutely unsurpassed cuisine. For complete information and illustrated literature, see your Travel Agent or write to Box 892, American Export Lines, 39 Broadway, New York 6, New York.

AMERICAN EXPORT LINES

POSTER FOR 'AN AFFAIR TO REMEMBER' (1957)

Much as one anticipates these two will be together, the film eludes expectations. / Man rechnet wohl damit, dass die beiden letztlich zueinanderfinden, doch der Film entzieht sich immer wieder solchen Erwartungen. / À l'heure des retrouvailles tant espérées, le film déjoue toutes nos attentes.

ADVERT FOR 'AN AFFAIR TO REMEMBER' (1957)

The power of the film grows out of its less predictable elements. / Die Stärke des Films sind die weniger vorhersehbaren Handlungselemente. / La force de ce film réside dans ses éléments les moins prévisibles.

STILL FROM 'THE PRIDE AND THE PASSION' (1957)
As a British officer in Spain, circa 1812, battling Napoleon's forces. / Als britischer Offizier in Spanien kämpft Grant um 1812 gegen die Truppen Napoleons. / En officier britannique combattant l'armée napoléonienne en Espagne, aux alentours de 1812.

STILL FROM 'THE PRIDE AND THE PASSION' (1957)
Grant's early training as a dancer and acrobat guides his assured footwork here. / Grants frühe Ausbildung als Tänzer und Akrobat verhalf ihm hier zu sicherer Beinarbeit. / Son expérience de jeunesse au sein d'une troupe de danseurs et d'acrobates lui confère un admirable jeu de jambes.

STILL FROM 'THE PRIDE AND THE PASSION' (1957)

A quiet moment with co-star Sophia Loren. / Ein stiller Augenblick mit Kollegin Sophia Loren. / Un moment de tranquillité avec sa partenaire Sophia Loren.

PORTRAIT FOR 'THE PRIDE AND THE PASSION' (1957)

The story's 'McGuffin' is an enormous cannon the French have abandoned. / Der ‚McGuffin' dieser Geschichte ist eine gewaltige Kanone, die von den Franzosen zurückgelassen wurde. / L'enjeu de la bataille est un énorme canon abandonné par les Français.

STILL FROM 'KISS THEM FOR ME' (1957)
With Jayne Mansfield and Leif Erickson in this farce about a hero's holiday. / Mit Jayne Mansfield und Leif Erickson in einem Lustspiel über einen Helden auf Landurlaub. / Avec Jayne Mansfield et Leif Erickson dans une farce narrant les frasques d'un héros en permission.

Reporter via telegram: 'HOW OLD CARY GRANT?'
Cary Grant's reply: 'OLD CARY GRANT FINE. HOW YOU?'

Reporter fragt im Telegramm: „ALTER CARY GRANT?" (gemeint: „ALTER [von] CARY GRANT?")
Cary Grants Antwort: „ALTER CARY GRANT WOHLAUF. UND SELBST?"

Télégramme d'un journaliste : « QUEL ÂGE CARY GRANT ? » (Littéralement : « COMMENT VIEUX CARY GRANT ? »)
Réponse de Cary Grant : « VIEUX CARY GRANT BIEN. ET VOUS ? »

STILL FROM 'KISS THEM FOR ME' (1957)
With Mansfield and Suzy Parker, as the holiday shenanigans grow complicated. / Mit Mansfield und Suzy Parker, als der Urlaubsunfug langsam außer Kontrolle gerät. / Avec Jayne Mansfield et Suzy Parker, lorsque ses frasques prennent une tournure inattendue.

STILL FROM 'INDISCREET' (1958)
Reunited with Ingrid Bergman, after the furor over her affair with Roberto Rossellini. / Wieder zusammen mit Ingrid Bergman, nach der Furore um ihre Affäre mit Roberto Rossellini. / Retrouvailles avec Ingrid Bergman après le scandale de sa liaison avec Roberto Rossellini.

"I've never been a joiner or a member of any particular social set, but I've been privileged to be a part of Hollywood's most glorious era."
Cary Grant, Honorary Oscar acceptance speech, 1970

„Ich war nie ein Vereinsmeier oder Mitglied einer bestimmten Gesellschaftsgruppe, aber ich hatte das Privileg, ein Teil der glorreichsten Ära Hollywoods sein zu dürfen."
Cary Grant, anlässlich der Verleihung des ‚Ehrenoscars' für sein Lebenswerk, 1970

ON THE SET OF 'INDISCREET' (1958)
Their chemistry rekindles, even without the help of director Stanley Donen (lower right). / Die alte Flamme lodert wieder auf – auch ohne den Beistand von Regisseur Stanley Donen (unten rechts). / L'alchimie opère à nouveau, même sans l'aide du réalisateur Stanley Donen (à droite).

« Je n'ai jamais été du genre à me revendiquer d'un groupe social particulier, mais j'ai eu le privilège de faire partie de Hollywood au moment de son apogée. »
Cary Grant lors de la remise de son oscar d'honneur, 1970

STILL FROM 'INDISCREET' (1958)
Bergman is a vacationing stage star, Grant a staid economist under her spell. / Bergman spielt einen Bühnenstar auf Urlaub und Grant einen gesetzten Volkswirt, der ihr verfällt. / Ingrid Bergman est une comédienne en vacances, Cary Grant un économiste coincé tombé sous son charme.

STILL FROM 'INDISCREET' (1958)
A crisp, rather Celtic soft-shoe from an old veteran of the Bob Pender troupe. / Ein flotter, etwas keltisch angehauchter Softshoe von einem alten Hasen aus der Bob-Pender-Truppe. / À mi-chemin entre les claquettes et la danse irlandaise, Grant retrouve l'agilité de ses débuts dans la troupe de Bob Pender.

STILL FROM 'HOUSEBOAT' (1958)
Hired as a nanny to his boy, Sophia Loren predictably wins Cary's heart. / Tom (Grant) engagiert Cinzia (Sophia Loren) als Kindermädchen für seinen Sohn, doch erwartungsgemäß erobert sie das Herz des Vaters. / Embauchée comme nounou de ses trois enfants, Sophia Loren conquiert évidemment le cœur du jeune veuf.

ON THE SET OF 'HOUSEBOAT' (1958)
A frank off-camera moment. Loren and Grant were lovers in real life for a time. / Eine Aussprache in der Drehpause. Loren und Grant waren eine Zeitlang auch privat liiert. / Moment d'intimité loin de la caméra. Sophia Loren et Cary Grant ont également eu une liaison dans la vraie vie.

PAGES 160/161
ON THE SET OF 'NORTH BY NORTHWEST' (1959)
Hitchcock's uncharacteristic use here of actual locations energizes this cross-country adventure. / Hitchcock verlieh seinem Abenteuer Schwung, indem er untypischerweise an Originalschauplätzen im ganzen Land drehte. / Le tournage en extérieur, inhabituel chez Hitchcock, insuffle une énergie à cette course poursuite à travers les États-Unis.

ROBE

E. F. HUTTON & COMPANY

STILL FROM 'NORTH BY NORTHWEST' (1959)
Romancing Eva Marie Saint. Grant's hair and suit match a shade of grey ideal for a man shorn of identity. / Roger turtelt mit Eve (Eva Marie Saint). Das Grau seiner Haare und seines Anzugs passen zu einem Menschen, der seiner Identität beraubt wurde. / Dans les bras d'Eva Marie Saint. Le gris de ses cheveux et de son costume convient parfaitement à un homme dépourvu d'identité.

STILL FROM 'NORTH BY NORTHWEST' (1959)
Innocent, but looking guilty as hell. Those light grey socks underscore the 'light step' of this comic thriller. / Der Anschein spricht hier deutlich gegen seine Unschuld. Die hellgrauen Socken unterstreichen die humoristische Seite dieses leichtfüßigen Thrillers. / Difficile d'avoir l'air moins innocent. Le gris clair de ses chaussettes souligne la légèreté de ce thriller comique.

STILL FROM 'NORTH BY NORTHWEST' (1959)
The film's ticklish and nightmarish qualities are laid bare in this literal cliffhanger. / Die alptraumhafte Spannung des Films legt auch in diesem Finale die Nerven blank – einem „Cliffhanger" im wahrsten Sinne des Wortes. / Le caractère cauchemardesque du film atteint son paroxysme dans cette scène au suspense vertigineux.

STILL FROM 'NORTH BY NORTHWEST' (1959)
A chase across America, under false identities and finally beneath the mythic figures atop Mount Rushmore. / Eine Hetzjagd unter falschem Namen quer durch die USA endet unter den Augen der mythischen Felsdenkmäler am Mount Rushmore. / Une course poursuite à travers l'Amérique qui s'achève sur les statues mythiques du Mont Rushmore.

STILL FROM 'OPERATION PETTICOAT' (1959)
Rescuing a submarine in wartime against comical odds, alongside Arthur O'Connell. / Allen komischen Widrigkeiten zum Trotz rettet Sherman (Grant) – hier mit Arthur O'Connell – während des Zweiten Weltkriegs ein angeschlagenes U-Boot. / Opération de sauvetage d'un sous-marin dans des conditions rocambolesques, aux côtés d'Arthur O'Connell.

"Cary Grant is a great comedian, a great light comedian. He's very good-looking, but he's also very funny. That makes a devastating combination, and that's why he's been a star so long."
Frank Capra

„Cary Grant ist ein großartiger Komiker, ein Meister der leichten Komödie. Er sieht sehr gut aus, aber er ist auch sehr witzig. Diese Kombination ist umwerfend, und deshalb ist er schon so lange ein Star."
Frank Capra

« Cary Grant est un grand comédien, un grand spécialiste de la comédie légère. Il est très bel homme, mais il est aussi très drôle. Cela donne un mélange irrésistible qui explique qu'il soit resté si longtemps célèbre. »
Frank Capra

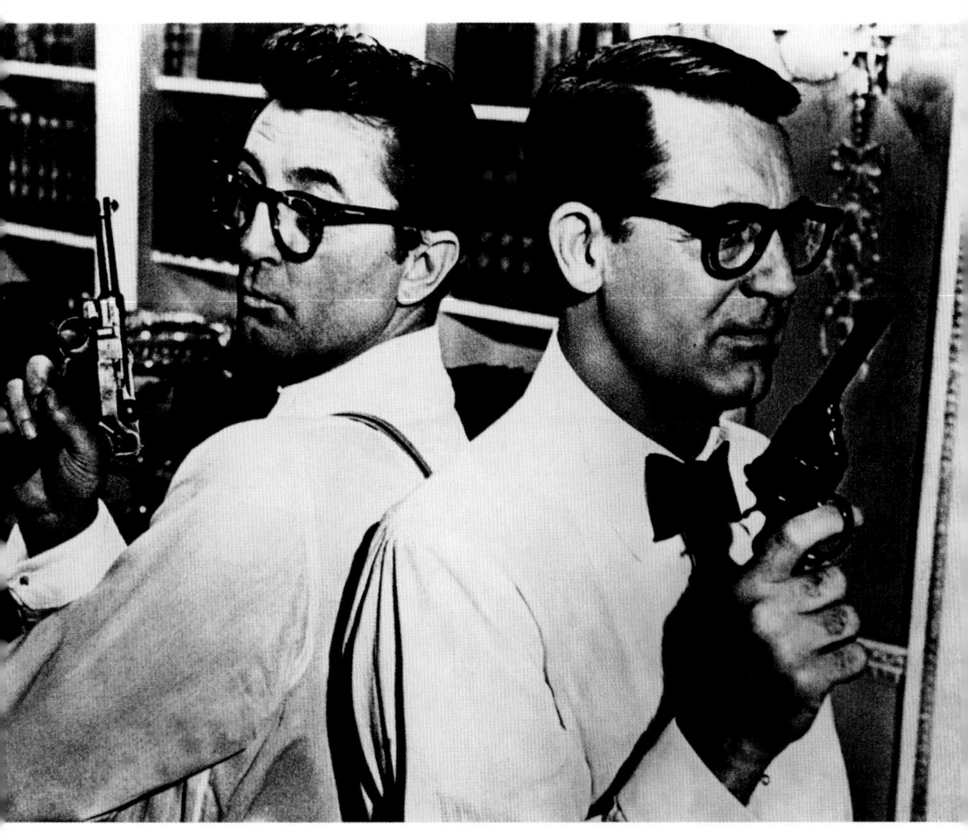

STILL FROM 'THE GRASS IS GREENER' (1960)
As an earl seeking satisfaction from an intrusive American houseguest (Robert Mitchum, left). / Grant spielt einen Adligen, der von einem aufdringlichen amerikanischen Hausgast (Robert Mitchum, links) Genugtuung verlangt. / En aristocrate tentant de se débarrasser d'un visiteur envahissant (Robert Mitchum, à gauche).

STILL FROM 'THAT TOUCH OF MINK' (1962)
An icon of suave dignity, he perpetually winds up stripped in public. / Die Ikone von Würde und Anstand steht doch immer wieder halbnackt in der Öffentlichkeit. / Bien que prototype du parfait gentleman, il se retrouve constamment dans des tenues indécentes.

ON THE SET OF 'THAT TOUCH OF MINK' (1962)
Lounging in comfortable style beside a lithe Doris Day. / Philip (Grant) fühlt sich sichtlich wohl an der Seite von Cathy (Doris Day). / Confortablement allongé aux côtés de Doris Day.

STILL FROM 'CHARADE' (1963)
A last hurrah for Hitchcock-like suspense, directed by Stanley Donen, opposite Audrey Hepburn. / Ein letzter Thriller im Hitchcock-Stil, allerdings unter der Regie von Stanley Donen und an der Seite von Audrey Hepburn. / En compagnie d'Audrey Hepburn dans un film de Stanley Donen au suspense digne de Hitchcock.

STILL FROM 'CHARADE' (1963)
Audrey Hepburn salves his wounds after he protects her from harm. Or is he deceiving her? / Reggie (Audrey Hepburn) versorgt Peters Wunden, nachdem er sie vor Schaden bewahrt hat. Oder treibt er etwa ein falsches Spiel mit ihr? / Soigné par Audrey Hepburn, qu'il vient de tirer d'un mauvais pas. À moins qu'il ne joue double jeu ?

"Cary Grant is by so far the best that there isn't anybody to be compared to him."
Howard Hawks

„Cary Grant ist bis heute der Beste, und es gibt niemanden, der ihm das Wasser reichen könnte."
Howard Hawks

« Cary Grant est de loin le meilleur ; personne ne peut se comparer à lui. »
Howard Hawks

STILL FROM 'CHARADE' (1963)
Grant may be shady here, but true menace comes courtesy of George Kennedy. / Grant spielt hier zwar eine undurchsichtige Figur, doch die eigentliche Bedrohung geht von Scobie (George Kennedy) aus. / Si Grant campe ici un personnage pour le moins louche, c'est de George Kennedy que vient la véritable menace.

STILL FROM 'FATHER GOOSE' (1964)
Prim schoolteacher Leslie Caron thinks she is dying of snakebite, but she's merely getting drunk. / Die spröde Lehrerin Catherine (Leslie Caron) glaubt, dass sie an einem Schlangenbiss stirbt, tatsächlich aber verspürt sie nur die Wirkung vom Alkohol. / L'institutrice guindée (Leslie Caron) attribue à une morsure de serpent des effets qui ne sont dus qu'à l'alcool.

PORTRAIT FOR 'FATHER GOOSE' (1964)
Unkempt and bestubbled, but ripe for reform in the thematic manner of 'The African Queen.' / Ungepflegt und unrasiert, aber durchaus besserungsfähig - in der Art von *African Queen*. / Négligé et mal rasé, mais prêt à se ranger comme Bogart dans *L'Odyssée de l'African Queen*.

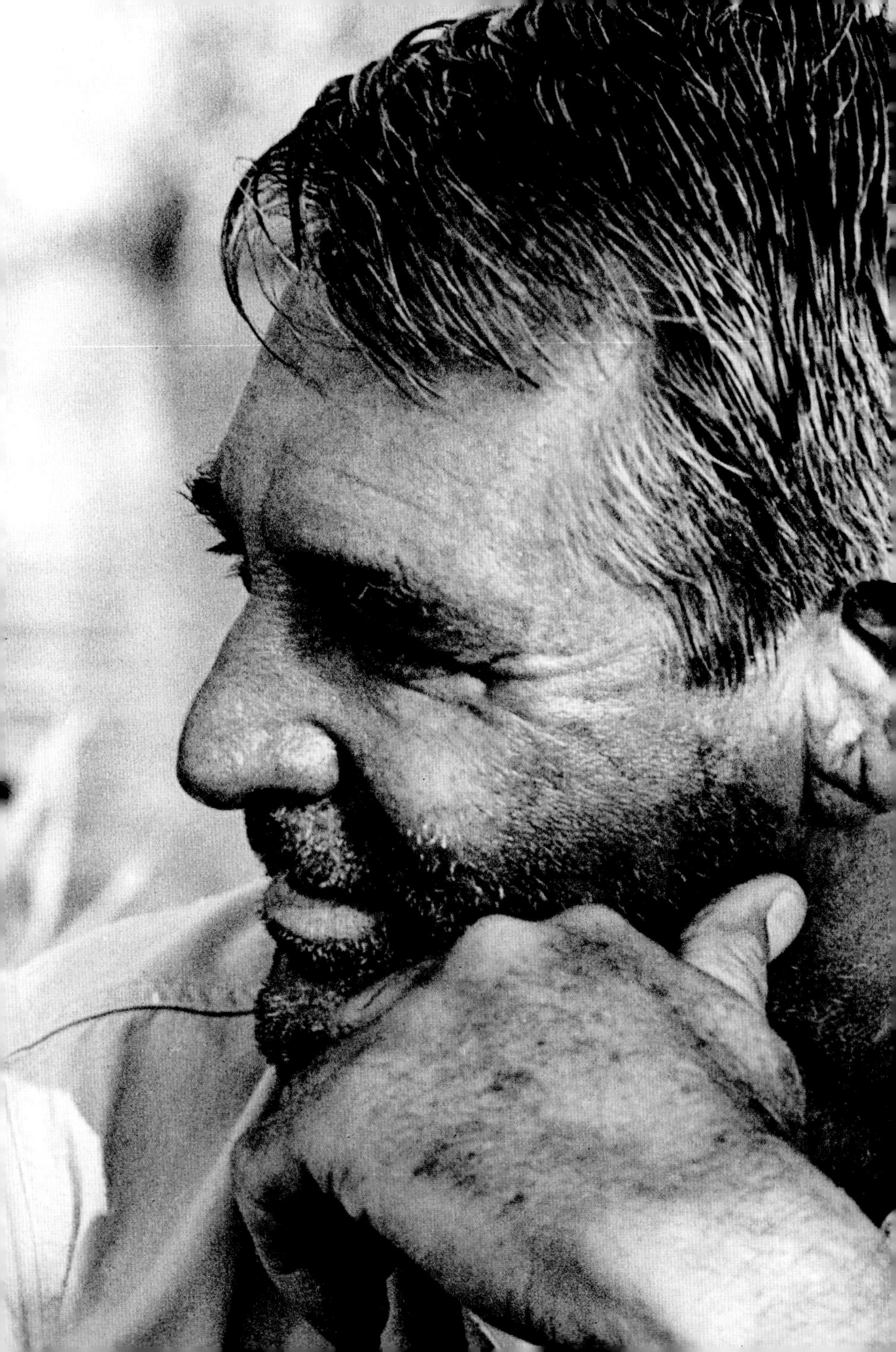

横断歩道で
止まろう
通
ノンスリップ
あ 46-73

STILL FROM 'WALK DON'T RUN' (1966)
Alongside Jim Hutton. Cary Grant ends as he began – athletic, upbeat, ever ready for fresh adventure. / An der Seite von Jim Hutton beendet Cary Grant seine Karriere so, wie er sie begann: athletisch, optimistisch und jederzeit bereit für ein neues Abenteuer. / Aux côtés de Jim Hutton, Cary Grant finit comme il a commencé : athlétique, optimiste, toujours prêt pour l'aventure.

PAGE 178
COVER OF 'MOVIE STORY MAGAZINE' (SEPTEMBER 1946)

ON THE SET OF 'WALK DON'T RUN' (1966)
His final film, a light-hearted comedy set at the 1964 Tokyo Olympics. He believed it was time to retire. / Sein letzter Film war eine unbeschwerte Komödie, die während der Olympischen Spiele von Tokio im Jahre 1964 spielt. / Son dernier film avant son départ en retraite, une comédie légère qui se déroule pendant les Jeux olympiques de Tokyo en 1964.

MOVIE STORY

MAGAZIN

SEPTEMBER

15c

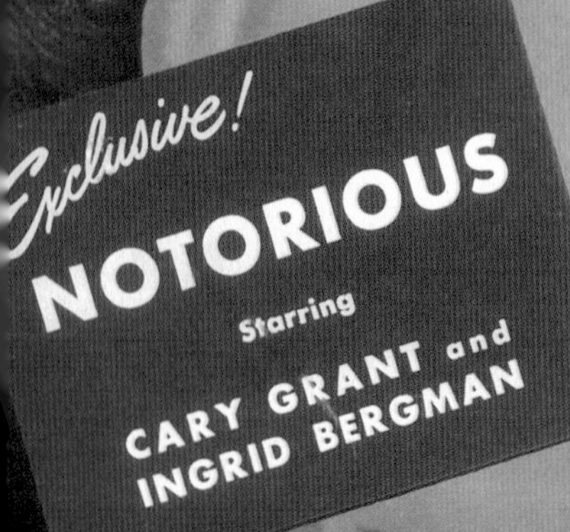

3

CHRONOLOGY

CHRONOLOGIE

CHRONOLOGIE

18 January 1904 Born Archibald Alexander Leach, at 15 Hughenden Rd., Bristol, England.

1914 His mother is wrongfully committed to a mental institution. He is told his mother has died.

March 1918 Expelled from Fairfield School and forges his father's signature on a document which allows him to join Bob Pender's Troupe of Acrobats.

July 1920–1924 Sails to America with Pender's Troupe, and travels America on the vaudeville circuit.

1925–1926 Employed by the Nightingale Players in England.

1927–1931 In the United States, has a success onstage in *Golden Dawn* (1927), which leads to other stage roles. Takes his first screen test in 1929, opposite Jeanette MacDonald.

November 1931 Signs contract with Paramount Pictures. Changes his name to Cary Grant.

1933 Shares a house with pal and fellow Paramount star Randolph Scott.

November 1933 Learns that his mother is alive in a mental institution. Grant suffers black depressions as a result of this discovery.

10 February 1934 Marries Virginia Cherrill.

26 March 1935 Divorces Virginia Cherrill.

2 December 1935 Father dies, owing to complications of alcoholism.

November 1936 As his 5-year contract expires, Grant announces his separation from Paramount. He makes a semi-exclusive arrangement with Columbia and RKO in 1937, and henceforth is primarily a freelance film star.

January 1941 Several of his relatives in Bristol are killed by Nazi bombs. Donates his fees for *The Philadelphia Story* to the British war drive.

26 June 1942 Officially becomes a US citizen, and legally changes his name to Cary Grant.

8 July 1942 Marries Barbara Hutton.

30 August 1945 Divorces Barbara Hutton.

25 December 1949 Marries Betsy Drake.

1952 Announces retirement from movies.

1955 Stars in Hitchcock's *To Catch a Thief*.

1957 Under the direction of psychiatrists, begins a three-year regimen taking supervised doses of LSD, then legal, as a therapeutic supplement.

14 August 1962 Divorces Betsy Drake.

22 July 1965 Marries Dyan Cannon.

26 February 1966 Birth of Grant's daughter, Jennifer.

15 July 1966 *Walk Don't Run*, his last film, is released. Grant is content to enjoy fatherhood.

21 March 1968 Divorces Dyan Cannon.

22 January 1973 His mother dies peacefully in Bristol.

11 April 1981 Marries Barbara Harris – they are together until his death.

29 November 1986 Dies suddenly at age 82 of a cerebral hemorrhage while visiting Davenport, Iowa as part of his popular tour, *An Evening with Cary Grant*.

COVER OF 'MOVIE STORY MAGAZINE' (JULY 1938)

THRILLING STORY VERSIONS OF ALL THE NEW PICTURES

JULY
NSC
1938

KATHARINE HEPBURN
CARY GRANT IN "HOLIDAY"

Katharine Hepburn
and Cary Grant
By Mozert

MARGARET SULLAVAN, JAMES STEWART IN "SHOPWORN ANGEL"
LUISE RAINER, MELVYN DOUGLAS IN "THE TOY WIFE"

THE BACHELOR AND THE BOBBY-SOXER

Starring

CARY GRANT, SHIRLEY TEMPLE

MYRNA LOY

AND OTHER NEW HIT FILMS STARRING LEW AYRES
BILL HOLDEN, JOAN CAULFIELD, FRANCHOT TONE
ANN SHERIDAN, LUCILLE BALL, ZACHARY SCOTT

Cary Grant and Shirley Temple

CHRONOLOGIE

18. Januar 1904 Er wird als Archibald Alexander Leach in der Hughenden Road Nr. 15 in Bristol, England, geboren.

1914 Seine Mutter wird zu Unrecht in eine Nervenheilanstalt eingewiesen. Ihm erzählt man, sie sei gestorben.

März 1918 Er wird von der Fairfield-Schule verwiesen und fälscht die Unterschrift seines Vaters auf einem Dokument, das ihm gestattet, der Akrobatentruppe von Bob Pender beizutreten.

Juli 1920–1924 Er reist mit der Pender-Truppe nach Amerika und tingelt dort durch die Varietés.

1925–1926 Er wird bei den Nightingale Players in England angestellt.

1927–1931 In den Vereinigten Staaten feiert er einen Bühnenerfolg mit *Golden Dawn* (1927) und erhält dadurch weitere Theaterrollen. Im Jahre 1929 spricht er zum ersten Mal für eine Filmrolle vor, an der Seite von Jeanette MacDonald.

November 1931 Er schließt einen Vertrag mit Paramount Pictures und nennt sich von nun an Cary Grant.

1933 Er teilt sich ein Haus mit seinem Freund und Kollegen Randolph Scott.

November 1933 Er erfährt, dass seine Mutter in einer Nervenklinik lebt, und leidet als Folge dieser Entdeckung unter schweren Depressionen.

10. Februar 1934 Er heiratet Virginia Cherrill.

26. März 1935 Er lässt sich von Virginia Cherrill scheiden.

2. Dezember 1935 Sein Vater stirbt an den Folgen seiner Trunksucht.

November 1936 Als sein Fünfjahresvertrag ausläuft, verkündet Grant, dass er sich von Paramount trennt. Er schließt 1937 halboffene Vereinbarungen mit Columbia und RKO und arbeitet fortan hauptsächlich als selbständiger Filmstar.

Januar 1941 Einige seiner Verwandten in Bristol werden bei deutschen Luftangriffen getötet.

COVER OF 'MOVIE STORY MAGAZINE' (AUGUST 1947)

Er spendet daraufhin seine Gage aus dem Film *The Philadelphia Story* (*Die Nacht vor der Hochzeit*) der britischen Kriegskasse.

26. Juni 1942 Er erhält die US-amerikanische Staatsbürgerschaft und ändert seinen Namen nun auch offiziell in Cary Grant um.

8. Juli 1942 Er heiratet Barbara Hutton.

30. August 1945 Er lässt sich von Barbara Hutton scheiden.

25. Dezember 1949 Er heiratet Betsy Drake.

1952 Er kündigt seinen Rückzug aus dem Filmgeschäft an.

1955 Er spielt die männliche Hauptrolle in Hitchcocks *To Catch a Thief* (*Über den Dächern von Nizza*).

1957 Beginnt unter ärztlicher Aufsicht eine dreijährige Therapie mit LSD.

14. August 1962 Er lässt sich von Betsy Drake scheiden.

22. Juli 1965 Er heiratet Dyan Cannon.

26. Februar 1966 Seine Tochter Jennifer wird geboren.

15. Juli 1966 *Walk Don't Run* (*Nicht so schnell, mein Junge*), sein letzter Film, kommt in die Kinos. Grant gibt sich damit zufrieden, fortan nur noch Vater zu spielen.

21. März 1968 Er lässt sich von Dyan Cannon scheiden.

22. Mai 1968 Er wird in den Vorstand des Kosmetikkonzerns Fabergé berufen.

22. Januar 1973 Seine Mutter stirbt friedlich in Bristol.

11. April 1981 Er heiratet Barbara Harris – sie bleiben zusammen, bis sein Tod sie scheidet.

29. November 1986 Er stirbt plötzlich und unerwartet im Alter von 82 an einer Gehirnblutung, während er sich im Rahmen seiner vielbesuchten Tournee *An Evening with Cary Grant* in der Stadt Davenport, Iowa, aufhält.

CHRONOLOGIE

18 janvier 1904 De son vrai nom Archibald Alexander Leach, il naît à Bristol, en Angleterre.

1914 On lui fait croire au décès de sa mère, internée à tort dans un asile psychiatrique.

Mars 1918 Renvoyé de l'école de Fairfield, il imite la signature de son père pour pouvoir rejoindre la troupe d'acrobates de Bob Pender.

Juillet 1920–1924 Part en Amérique pour une tournée des music-halls avec la troupe de Pender.

1925–1926 Employé par la troupe des Nightingale Players en Angleterre.

1927-1931 Aux États-Unis, premier succès théâtral avec la pièce *Golden Dawn* (1927), qui lui permet de décrocher d'autres rôles. Tourne son premier bout d'essai en 1929 avec Jeanette MacDonald.

Novembre 1931 Signe un contrat avec la Paramount. Adopte son nom de scène, Cary Grant.

1933 Partage une maison avec son ami Randolph Scott, autre star de la Paramount.

Novembre 1933 Apprend que sa mère est toujours en vie dans un asile psychiatrique, ce qui le plonge dans une profonde dépression.

10 février 1934 Épouse Virginia Cherrill.

26 mars 1935 Divorce de Virginia Cherrill.

2 décembre 1935 Son père succombe à des complications dues à l'alcoolisme.

Novembre 1936 À l'expiration de son contrat de 5 ans, il annonce son départ de la Paramount. En 1937, il signe un contrat semi-exclusif avec Columbia et RKO et travaille principalement à titre indépendant.

Janvier 1941 À Bristol, plusieurs membres de sa famille sont tués lors des bombardements allemands. Il fait don de son cachet d'*Indiscrétions* pour contribuer à l'effort de guerre anglais.

26 juin 1942 Obtient la nationalité américaine et change officiellement de nom pour devenir Cary Grant.

8 juillet 1942 Épouse Barbara Hutton.

30 août 1945 Divorce de Barbara Hutton.

25 décembre 1949 Épouse Betsy Drake.

1952 Annonce qu'il arrête le cinéma.

1955 Joue le rôle principal dans *La Main au collet* d'Alfred Hitchcock.

1957 Des psychiatres lui prescrivent une cure à base de doses de LSD contrôlées qui durera trois ans.

14 août 1962 Divorce de Betsy Drake.

22 juillet 1965 Épouse Dyan Cannon.

26 février 1966 Naissance de sa fille Jennifer.

15 juillet 1966 Sortie de son dernier film, *Rien ne sert de courir*. Se consacre aux joies de la paternité.

21 mars 1968 Divorce de Dyan Cannon.

22 mai 1968 Nommé au Conseil d'administration du géant des cosmétiques Fabergé.

22 janvier 1973 Sa mère décède à Bristol.

11 avril 1981 Épouse Barbara Harris, avec laquelle il restera jusqu'à sa mort.

29 novembre 1986 Succombe brusquement à une hémorragie cérébrale à l'âge de 82 ans alors qu'il est de passage à Davenport, dans l'Iowa, dans le cadre de sa célèbre tournée *An Evening with Cary Grant*.

COVER OF 'MOVIE STORY MAGAZINE' (OCTOBER 1944)

OCTOBER
15c

I'D MARRY YOU, ERNIE---IF I HAD THE CHANCE"

ARY GRANT AND JANE WYATT IN A SCENE FROM NONE BUT THE LONELY HEART

THIS BIG RKO PRODUCTION COMPLETE IN THIS ISSUE FROM THE NOVEL BY RICHARD LLEWELLYN, AUTHOR OF HOW GREEN WAS MY VALLEY

R K O RADIO FILMS S.A. Présente

KATHARINE HEPBURN - CARY GRAN

b. lancy

R K O RADIO FILMS

L'IMPOSSIBLE MONSIEUR BÉBÉ

Mise en scène de HOWARD HAWKS

R. K. O. RADIO FILMS S.A. 52, Champs Elysées. Paris. Bal. 54-55 et la suite

4

FILMOGRAPHY

FILMOGRAFIE

FILMOGRAPHIE

Singapore Sue (1932)
As Sailor (uncredited)/Matrose (ungenannt)/ en marin (non crédité). Director/Regie/réalisateur: Casey Robinson. (Short/Kurzfilm/court métrage.)

This Is the Night (fr. *La Belle Nuit*, 1932)
Stephen. Director/Regie/réalisateur: Frank Tuttle.

Sinners in the Sun (1932)
Ridgeway. Director/Regie/réalisateur: Alexander Hall.

Merrily We Go to Hell (dt. *Geh' und lieb' und leide!*, 1932)
Charlie Baxter 'DeBrion'. Director/Regie/réalisateur: Dorothy Arzner.

Devil and the Deep (dt. *Die Frau im U-Boot* [aka *Teufel der Tiefsee*], fr. *Le Démon du sous-marin*, 1932)
Lieutenant Jaeckel. Director/Regie/réalisateur: Marion Gering.

Blonde Venus (fr. *La Vénus blonde*, 1932)
Nick Townsend. Director/Regie/réalisateur: Josef von Sternberg.

Hot Saturday (1932)
Romer Sheffield. Director/Regie/réalisateur: William A. Seiter.

Madame Butterfly (1932)
Lieutenant B. F. Pinkerton. Director/Regie/réalisateur: Marion Gering.

She Done Him Wrong (dt. *Sie tat ihm unrecht*, fr. *Lady Lou*, 1933)
Captain/Capitaine Cummings. Director/Regie/réalisateur: Lowell Sherman.

The Eagle and the Hawk (fr. *L'Aigle et le faucon*, 1933)
Henry Crocker. Director/Regie/réalisateur: Stuart Walker.

The Woman Accused (fr. *Celle qu'on accuse*, 1933)
Jeffrey Baxter. Director/Regie/réalisateur: Paul Sloane.

Gambling Ship (1933)
Ace Corbin. Directors: Louis J. Gasnier, Max Marcin.

I'm No Angel (dt. *Ich bin kein Engel*, fr. *Je ne suis pas un ange*, 1933)
Jack Clayton. Director/Regie/réalisateur: Wesley Ruggles

Alice in Wonderland (fr. *Alice au pays des merveilles*, 1933)
The Mock Turtle/Die „falsche Schildkröte"/« La tortue ». Director/Regie/réalisateur: Norman Z. McLeod.

Thirty Day Princess (dt. *Prinzessin für 30 Tage*, fr. *Princesse par intérim*, 1934)
Porter Madison III. Director/Regie/réalisateur: Marion Gering.

Born to Be Bad (1934)
Malcolm Trevor. Director/Regie/réalisateur: Lowell Sherman.

Kiss and Make-Up (dt. *Küsse und Schminke* [aka *Tempel der Schönheit/Wie werde ich jung und schön?*], 1934)
Dr. Maurice Loman. Director/Regie/réalisateur: Harlan Thompson.

Ladies Should Listen (fr. *Les femmes devraient écouter*, 1934)
Julian De Lussac. Director/Regie/réalisateur: Frank Tuttle.

Enter Madame (fr. *Caprice de femme*, 1935)
Gerald Fitzgerald. Director/Regie/réalisateur: Elliott Nugent.

Wings in the Dark (fr. *Les Ailes dans l'ombre*, 1935)
Ken Gordon. Director/Regie/réalisateur: James Flood.

The Last Outpost (dt. *Das letzte Fort*, fr. *Intelligence Service*, 1935)
Michael Andrews. Directors: Charles Barton, Louis J. Gasnier.

Sylvia Scarlett (1935)
Jimmy Monkley. Director/Regie/réalisateur: George Cukor.

The Amazing Quest of Ernest Bliss (fr. *La Chasse aux millions*, 1936)
Ernest Bliss. Director/Regie/réalisateur: Alfred Zeisler.

Big Brown Eyes (dt. *Große braune Augen*, fr. *Empreintes digitales*, 1936)
Danny Barr. Director/Regie/réalisateur: Raoul Walsh.

Suzy (dt. *Bigamie*, fr. *Une belle blonde*, 1936)
Captain/Capitaine Andre Charville. Director/Regie/réalisateur: George Fitzmaurice.

Wedding Present (fr. *Bonne blague* [aka *Cadeau de mariage*], 1936)
Charlie. Director/Regie/réalisateur: Richard Wallace.

When You're in Love (fr. *Le Cœur en fête*, 1937)
Jimmy Hudson. Director/Regie/réalisateur: Robert Riskin.

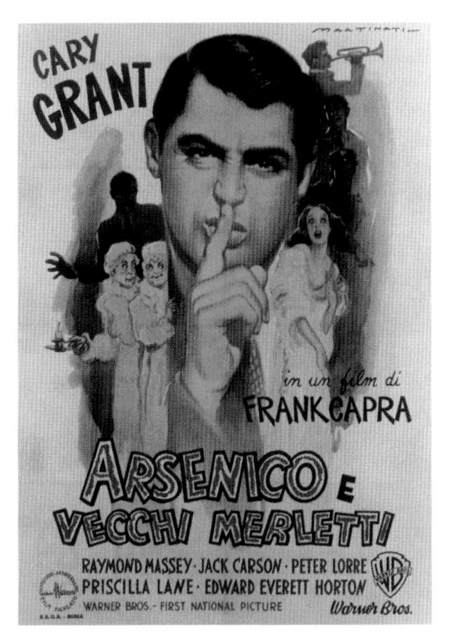

Topper (dt. *Zwei Engel ohne Flügel* [aka *Das blonde Gespenst*], fr. *Le Couple invisible*, 1937)
George Kerby. Director/Regie/réalisateur: Norman Z. McLeod.

The Toast of New York (dt. *Geldrausch*, fr. *L'Or et la femme*, 1937)
Nicholas 'Nick' Boyd. Director/Regie/réalisateur: Roland V. Lee.

The Awful Truth (dt. *Die schreckliche Wahrheit*, fr. *Cette sacrée vérité*, 1937)
Jerry Warriner. Director/Regie/réalisateur: Leo McCarey.

Bringing Up Baby (dt. *Leoparden küßt man nicht*, fr. *L'Impossible Monsieur Bébé*, 1938)
Dr. David Huxley. Director/Regie/réalisateur: Howard Hawks.

Holiday (dt. *Die Schwester der Braut*, fr. *Vacances*, 1938)
John 'Johnny' Case. Director/Regie/réalisateur: George Cukor.

In Name Only (dt. *Nur dem Namen nach*, fr. *L'Autre*, 1939)
Alec Walker. Director/Regie/réalisateur: John Cromwell.

Gunga Din (dt. *Aufstand in Sidi Hakim*, 1939)
Sergeant Archibald Cutter.
Director/Regie/réalisateur: George Stevens.

Only Angels Have Wings (dt. *SOS Feuer an Bord* [aka *Flugpioniere in Not*], fr. *Seuls les anges ont des ailes*, 1939)
Geoff Carter. Director/Regie/réalisateur: Howard Hawks.

His Girl Friday (dt. *Sein Mädchen für besondere Fälle*, fr. *La Dame du vendredi*, 1940)

Walter Burns. Director/Regie/réalisateur: Howard Hawks.

My Favorite Wife (dt. *Meine liebste Frau* [aka *Meine Lieblingsfrau*], fr. *Mon épouse favorite*, 1940)
Nick Arden. Director/Regie/réalisateur: Garson Kanin.

The Howards of Virginia (fr. *Howard le révolté*, 1940)
Matt Howard. Director/Regie/réalisateur: Frank Lloyd.

The Philadelphia Story (dt. *Die Nacht vor der Hochzeit*, fr. *Indiscrétions*, 1940)
C. K. Dexter Haven. Director/Regie/réalisateur: George Cukor.

Penny Serenade (dt. *Akkorde der Liebe*, fr. *La Chanson du passé*, 1941)
Roger Adams. Director/Regie/réalisateur: George Stevens.

Suspicion (dt. *Verdacht*, fr. *Soupçons*, 1941)
Johnnie Aysgarth. Director/Regie/réalisateur: Alfred Hitchcock.

The Talk of the Town (dt. *Zeuge der Anklage*, fr. *La Justice des hommes*, 1942)
Leopold Dilg/Joseph. Director/Regie/réalisateur: George Stevens.

Once Upon a Honeymoon (dt. *Es waren einmal Flitterwochen*, fr. *Lune de miel mouvementée*, 1942)
Patrick 'Pat' O'Toole. Director/Regie/réalisateur: Leo McCarey.

Mr. Lucky (1943)
Joe Adams aka/alias Joe Bascopolous.
Director/Regie/réalisateur: H. C. Potter.

Destination Tokyo (dt. *Bestimmung Tokio* [aka *Ein gefährlicher Auftrag*], 1943)
Captain/Capitaine Cassidy.
Director/Regie/réalisateur: Delmer Daves.

Once Upon a Time (dt. *Pinky und Curly*, 1944)
Jerry Flynn. Director/Regie/réalisateur: Alexander Hall.

None But the Lonely Heart (fr. *Rien qu'un cœur solitaire*, 1944)
Ernie Mott. Director/Regie/réalisateur: Clifford Odets.

Arsenic and Old Lace (dt. *Arsen und Spitzenhäubchen*, fr. *Arsenic et vieilles dentelles*, 1944)
Mortimer Brewster. Director/Regie/réalisateur: Frank Capra.

Night and Day (dt. *Nacht und Tag* [aka *Tag und Nacht denk' ich an dich*], fr. *Nuit et jour*, 1946)
Cole Porter. Director/Regie/réalisateur: Michael Curtiz.

Notorious (dt. *Berüchtigt* [aka *Weißes Gift*], fr. *Les Enchaînés*, 1946)
T. R. Devlin . Director/Regie/réalisateur: Alfred Hitchcock.

The Bachelor and the Bobby-Soxer (dt. *Der Backfisch und der Junggeselle* [aka *So einfach ist die Liebe nicht*], fr. *Deux sœurs vivaient en paix*, 1947)
Richard Nugent. Director/Regie/réalisateur: Irving Reis.

The Bishop's Wife (dt. *Jede Frau braucht einen Engel* [aka *Engel sind überall*], fr. *Honni soit qui mal y pense*, 1947)
Dudley. Director/Regie/réalisateur: Henry Koster.

Mr. Blandings Builds His Dream House (dt. *Nur meiner Frau zuliebe* [aka *Madame wünscht sich ein Haus*], fr. *Un million clefs en main*, 1948)
Jim Blandings. Director/Regie/réalisateur: H. C. Potter.

Every Girl Should Be Married (dt. *Jedes Mädchen müßte heiraten* [aka *Was jedes Mädchen möchte*], fr. *La Course au mari*, 1948)
Dr. Madison W. Brown. Director/Regie/réalisateur: Don Hartman.

I Was a Male War Bride (dt. *Ich war eine männliche Kriegsbraut*, fr. *Allez coucher ailleurs*, 1949)
Captain/Capitain Henri Rochard. Director/Regie/réalisateur: Howard Hawks.

Crisis (dt. *Hexenkessel*, fr. *Cas de conscience*, 1950)
Dr. Eugene Norland Ferguson. Director/Regie/réalisateur: Richard Brooks.

People Will Talk (fr. *On murmure dans la ville*, 1951)
Dr. Noah Praetorius. Director/Regie/réalisateur: Joseph L. Mankiewicz.

Room for One More (dt. *Vater werden ist nicht schwer*, fr. *Cette sacrée famille*, 1952)
George 'Poppy' Rose. Director/Regie/réalisateur: Norman Taurog.

Monkey Business (dt. *Liebling, ich werde jünger*, fr. *Chérie, je me sens rajeunir*, 1952)
Dr. Barnaby Fulton. Director/Regie/réalisateur: Howard Hawks.

Dream Wife (dt. *Du und keine andere*, fr. *La Femme rêvée*, 1953)
Clemson Reade. Director/Regie/réalisateur: Sidney Sheldon.

To Catch a Thief (dt. *Über den Dächern von Nizza*, fr. *La Main au collet*, 1955)
John Robie . Director/Regie/réalisateur: Alfred Hitchcock.

An Affair to Remember (dt. *Die große Liebe meines Lebens*, fr. *Elle et lui*, 1957)
Nickie Ferrante. Director/Regie/réalisateur: Leo McCarey.

The Pride and the Passion (dt. *Stolz und Leidenschaft*, fr. *Orgueil et passion*, 1957)
Anthony. Director/Regie/réalisateur: Stanley Kramer.

Kiss Them for Me (fr. *Embrasse-la pour moi*, 1957)
Commander/Commandant Andy Crewson. Director/Regie/réalisateur: Stanley Donen.

Indiscreet (dt. *Indiskret*, fr. *Indiscret*, 1958)
Philip Adams. Director/Regie/réalisateur: Stanley Donen.

Houseboat (dt. *Hausboot*, fr. *La Péniche du bonheur*, 1958)
Tom Winters. Director/Regie/réalisateur: Melville Shavelson.

North by Northwest (dt. *Der unsichtbare Dritte*, fr. *La Mort aux trousses*, 1959)
Roger O. Thornhill . Director/Regie/réalisateur: Alfred Hitchcock.

Operation Petticoat (dt. *Unternehmen Petticoat*, fr. *Opération jupons*, 1959)
Lieutenant Commander/Lieutenant-commandant Matt T. Sherman. Director/Regie/réalisateur: Blake Edwards.

The Grass Is Greener (dt. *Vor Hausfreunden wird gewarnt*, fr. *Ailleurs, l'herbe est plus verte*, 1960)
Earl Victor Rhyall. Director/Regie/réalisateur: Stanley Donen.

That Touch of Mink (dt. *Ein Hauch von Nerz*, fr. *Un soupçon de vison*, 1962)
Philip Shayne. Director/Regie/réalisateur: Delbert Mann.

Charade (1963)
Peter Joshua. Director/Regie/réalisateur: Stanley Donen.

Father Goose (dt. *Der große Wolf ruft*, fr. *Grand méchant loup appelle*, 1964)
Walter Christopher Eckland. Director/Regie/réalisateur: Ralph Nelson.

Walk Don't Run (dt. *Nicht so schnell, mein Junge*, fr. *Rien ne sert de courir*, 1966)
Sir William Rutland. Director/Regie/réalisateur: Charles Walters.

BIBLIOGRAPHY

Bueher, Beverley Bare: *Cary Grant, A Bio-Bibliography*. Greenwood Press, 1990.
Deschner, Donald: *The Films of Cary Grant*. Citadel Press, 1973.
Donaldson, Maureen & Royce, William: *An Affair to Remember*. Putnams, 1989.
Eliot, Marc: *Cary Grant, A Biography*. Harmony Books, 2004.
Cary Grant: In the Spotlight. Galley Press / Mayflower Books, 1980.
Godfrey, Lionel: *Cary Grant, The Light Touch*. St. Martin's Press, 1981.
Govoni, Albert: *Cary Grant, An Unauthorized Biography*. Henry Regnery Co., 1971.
Guthrie, Lee: *The Life and Loves of Cary Grant*. Drake, 1977.
Harris, Warren G.: *Cary Grant, A Touch of Elegance*. Doubleday, 1987.
Higham, Charles & Moseley, Roy: *Cary Grant, The Lonely Heart*. Harcourt Brace Jovanovich, 1989.
McCann, Graham: *Cary Grant, A Class Apart*. Columbia University Press, 1996
McIntosh, William Currie & Weaver, William: *The Private Cary Grant*. Sidgwick & Jackson, 1983.
Nelson, Nancy: *Evenings with Cary Grant*. William Morrow, 1991.
Schickel, Richard: *Cary Grant: A Celebration*. Applause Books, 1999.
Torregrossa, Richard: *Cary Grant: A Celebration of Style*. Bulfinch, 2006.
Trescott, Pamela: *Cary Grant, His Movies and His Life*. Acropolis Books, 1987.
Vermilye, Jerry: *Cary Grant*. Galahad, 1973.
Wansell, Geoffrey: *Haunted Idol, The Story of the Real Cary Grant*. William Morrow, 1984.
Wansell, Geoffrey: *Cary Grant, Dark Angel*. Arcade, 1996.

IMPRINT

Hohenzollernring 53, D-50672 Köln
www.taschen.com

Editor/Picture Research/Layout: Paul Duncan/Wordsmith Solutions
Editorial Coordination: Martin Holz, Cologne
Production Coordination: Nadia Najm and Horst Neuzner, Cologne
German Translation: Thomas J. Kinne, Nauheim
French Translation: Anne Le Bot, Paris
Multilingual Production: www.arnaudbriand.com, Paris
Typeface Design: Sense/Net, Andy Disl and Birgit Reber, Cologne

Printed in Italy
ISBN 978-3-8228-2212-8